THE WOK

Gary Lee

A Nitty Gritty Book*
Published by
Nitty Gritty Productions
P.O. Box 5457
Concord, California 94524

*Nitty Gritty Books - Trademark
Owned by Nitty Gritty Productions
Concord, California

ISBN 0-911954-06-6

Library of Congress Catalog Card Number: 79-19094

Illustrated by Mike Nelson

DEDICATIONS

I did not write this book by myself alone, without many persons' efforts and influences, it would still be a dream.

I sincerely dedicate it to:

To readers and friends of my cooking class: who like and enjoy cooking.

To my family members: with them I was beloved and raised. Keep on wishing; till we meet again!

To my teachers and friends: how I wish to have had all of you near with me when I was writing. You surely would have made this book more interesting.

To those who wished me bad: I thank you too, for it was a challenge from which I have benefited. As I was a rough stone, by constant polishing of wind and water, I am turning round and shining.

To Mr. and Mrs. John Owen Lloyd, C.B.E.: multilingual, phraseologists, and gourmets, for their encouragement in the writing of this book.

To Mike: for his artful drawing by hand with mind, which gives life to this book.

To James Murray, Esq., C.M.G.: He likes our Chinese congee and walks miles every morning. He leaves the Jaguar behind with the bacon and eggs. Congee is a kind of rice-soup of Chinese breakfast. Jaguar is the car he has. He is famous in this town for his daily walking even on raining days.

To Christine and Adrienne: for their intelligent corrections of mistakes, leaving in my writing a strong Chinnese seasoning.

To Ed: for his tedious job in editing and valuable suggestions.

To Annie and Chan: for changing my mind.

To Rev. and Mrs. Chee Wu: for changing my life.

To my loving daughters Vida and Linda: to them this little book will be a souvenir, their helping me in childhood will always be remembered.

To my darling wife Hedy: a girl I promised to make as a queen, turned out a slave following me wandering around the world! Brought me to a land of expensive living but free thinking!

Gary Lee
San Francisco, 1970

TABLE OF CONTENTS

給

海外僑胞、讀者们。

　　這本小冊，並非吹嘘本人
的技能與智識。唯一的目的，是
讓外人認識。"中國的烹飪"，
絕非任何國，堪與我们相比。
　　也為了"烹飪"順便介紹給外人，
"黃帝的子孫"，有傳統的智慧與美德。

匆匆作完，敬請指教。

李一中 (行浩)
客振三藩市。
一九七〇

TO MY OVERSEAS CHINESE FRIENDS:

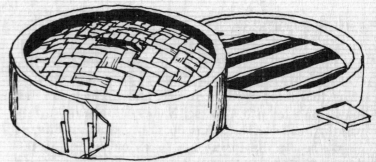

When living happily in a foreign country, what can you offer to your friends? I think the easiest and best thing is to cook them a Chinese dinner. I wish that you would always cook a good dinner, not only to let others respect our Chinese cooking art, but to also let your children learn our national culture. I regretfully say that many Chinese housewives still speak poorly in English, perhaps because they just don't want to learn it, yet in a short period of months, they learn to serve a TV dinner!

This book is written for the beginner, to follow the basic cooking techniques very seriously. All the recipes might seem too simple, yet they are so important as they serve to help you understand "why", even though you might already know "how".

I am going to write another cook book about fancy dishes, such as Milk Chinese-fried, and Bean Curd of Chicken's Brains (which has neither bean curd nor brains, but it tastes like brains and looks like mashed bean curd -- and is made from minced chicken breast).

To cook a fancy dish is just as easy as cooking a normal dish, providing you know how to do each cooking technique. In the coming fancy recipes, no more explanation will be given, no measurement of seasonings, only special tricks will be hinted at in simple words.

If you agree that cooking is an art and science, I hope you can find something useful in this book, and be happy in your kitchen. Don't be hesitant in answering all questions from your friends, as any art or science deserves to be shared with anyone who is interested.

One thing of which I am very sure is that one who likes to cook is mostly unselfish, hospitable, punctual, neat, considerate, and peaceful. This is the kind of person we need now in the world.

1

CHINESE COOKING

To cook is a necessity; to know how is an art. Speaking of arts, as I am Chinese, please allow me to claim that there are at least three arts in which no other may compare with Chinese. Namely: literature, brush-painting, and cooking. This does not mean that Chinese are the best in these three arts, because there is a big difference between Chinese and non-Chinese. To use literature as an educational tool, Chinese is clumsy, i.e. type-writing and filing systems. But the beauty of the Chinese literature is unexplainable to people who have not been trained to understand it. This is because we have completely different kinds of words. Each word is a character which is so visually representational that when you see the word "smile" you feel gay, and when you see the word "cry" you feel sad. To use painting to record a real-life picture, Chinese are never the best -- you may judge that an old mountain man is not proportionately the size of a giant tree, however, if you ever saw a good Chinese artist finish a brush-painting, you would be amazed at his thoughtful confidence in his brush. Each brush-painting is as a personal signature; unretouchable and unimitative.

To compare cooking between Chinese and non-Chinese, is to compare the East and West. Chinese have all meats cut to bite-size, while others serve a steak of l6 oz. Chinese use only a pair of chopsticks, while Westerners have forks and knives for fish and meat. Soup served last vs. soup served first. Confucious mentioned to his pupils "No speech during the meal", while others like to deliver a long speech at a formal dinner. Chinese cook most food in a wok vs. others in a flat bottom pan.

In Chinese cooking each dish shows its own character for there are more than thirty kinds of cooking techniques to be adopted. Others care less for cooking than for decorating -- from the table arrangement to the dish. Garnish any dish with parsley, lemon wedge, tomato, cucumber, boiled eggs. In conclusion, Chinese cook for enjoyment of the food while Westerners cook for entertainment or formality. For instance, Chinese prefer light at a dinner party while Westerners dim it with candle light. To Westerners the mood may be more important than the food.

It was around the late 1950's that the famous Saturday Evening Post had an interesting column called "The Perfect Squelch". I still remember one of the best:

A lady went to buy a horse and told the horse dealer, "I am looking for a horse which must be beautiful and young; I like to gallop every afternoon into town; it must be strong enough to help in my husband's field work; it must be tame as my daughter is taking riding lessons. At a reasonable price, of course." The horse dealer asked in a soft voice, "Do you also want to milk her, M'am?" My cooking ability and recipes have impressed many people, yet many times have failed as someone demanded a cooking system that is quick, easy, economical, delicious, and, of course, healthful! I have used the horse story many times as my reply for, of course, nothing can be all things to all people.

Chinese serve no dessert at home, and Westerners serve only one dessert daily because they are on a diet. Chinese use sugar in almost every dish (very little for harmonizing purpose) and cook with oil while Westerners take artificial sugar and cook with butter. I have no intention to offend non-Chinese cooking. As I have mentioned to use cooking for entertaining at a formal event, the Westerners are really the best. Each guest has one glass for water, one sherry glass with the soup, a white wine glass with the seafood, a red wine glass with the meat, and a champagne glass with the dessert or for a toast, several pairs of forks and knives; besides the rolls, breads, biscuits, candies, salt and pepper, butter and jam, as well as the butter knife and jam spoon, etc. The setting is really impressive, but if you want to enjoy food, my dear reader, please join me in Chinese cooking. You will be surprised that Chinese cooking in some ways is really much simpler than you imagine and you can apply all these Chinese cooking techniques to your own cooking. It can improve your cooking style no matter how original it may be.

The Great Master Confucius agreed that "a gentleman is fond of prosperity, but achieves it justly". As an author, I wish this cook book to be a bestseller, but I confess that there is no miracle, only some technology, a few secrets and tricks, and whether or not they work will depend on your patience and practice.

3

LET'S GO TO THE KITCHEN

In the planning of this cookbook, the publisher suggested to me that I write more about the simpler dishes in Chinese cooking. After I started, I found out that there is only one choice; the right way or the wrong way.

Knowing how, most Chinese dishes are both easy and hard at the same time. There is only one difference between complicated and uncomplicated - the time consumed in preparing or cooking.

Let's take the right way. First, let's check your kitchen. We need some minimum requirements in tools to start. I never had a chance to play golf, but I know that you cannot play golf with only one club - even though you might be as good a player as Bob Hope!

It is puzzling to me to see the cookware that is on the market. I wonder if their designers ever practiced cooking or not? Cookware is to be used, not only to be displayed, unless you are a cookware salesman.

A wok, if you have one, is a good first choice for Chinese-frying. A skillet is a second choice for Chinese-frying. A frying pan, if the depth is less than 2 inches, will be good for shallow-frying. It is also a third choice for Chinese-frying.

An old Chinese proverb says, "To have the job well done, first sharpen the tools." This carries even a little bit further as you not only need the tools, but they must be sharp. In the case of cooking, especially in Chinese cooking, the right tools are very important.

The wok is a very versatile kitchen tool. If there were any kitchenware competitions, it would deserve a gold medal.

It is ideal for deep-frying, as its somewhat conical shape requires less oil than a flat bottom frying pan, gives more depth and frying surface; and, more important, it has a larger capacity on the upper end. Therefore, the oil level may rise as the raw materials are underneath frying, but with little chance for the oil to flood out, as usually happens with an ordinary frying pan.

The wok does not need chemical treatment. Under proper use, food does not stick. No special cooking spoons are required, no heat limit.

Had engineers used a wok, and seen a professional Chinese cook clean a burned wok, the self-cleaning oven would have been invented a long time ago. You just burn it at a high temperature till clean.

As the bottom is round with no corners, you may

make an omelet or crepes suzette to any size by tilting the wok around.

A whole fish may be fried with little oil in a wok, and it is very simple to fry a large fish in a small wok. To fry a 15 inch fish in a 12 inch western frying pan is almost impossible without breaking the fish in half.

As a steamer it works well down to the last spoonfuls of water. Its price is reasonable, but that lady who was looking for a horse still will not like the wok! Do you know why? – Because the wok is not beautiful!

I have no intention of selling you a wok; therefore, let me tell you some of the disadvantages of using one.

First, it works well with a gas burner, while an electric one is not quite as satisfactory. I also do not wish to convince you to switch from electricity to gas - here are some hints for using the wok on an electric burner:

If your wok has the wooden single side handle, it will not balance without the adapter ring. The rings make a compromise and fit most electric ranges. The important thing is that the wok has direct contact with the burner.

If it does not quite touch the burner, the heat transfer will be too low for some dishes that need high temperatures. A solution is to use some metal disks or squares that are not painted (galvanized will work) to shim up until direct contact between pan and burner is made. This will insure high temperatures and is completely safe. Just be sure to remember that the shims will be as hot as the pan itself.

PAN FOR DEEP FRYING

I had never measured the depth of my small wok pan and was astonished to find that it is only three inches in depth. I am able to fill it up to two-thirds full of oil for a sizeable frying job. However, I would not advise you to try this. The most you should fill your wok is less than 1 1/2" with oil. If you don't have a special pan for deep frying, use an ordinary cooking pan with a depth of at least five inches. The smaller the diameter of the pan is, the less oil you will need to fill it to a depth of about two inches.

CHOPPING BLOCK

Cutting board or chopping block — Although you may not chop on your cutting board, you may cut on a chopping block.

The typical Chinese chopping block is a round cross section piece of a tree trunk. A soft wood is preferable. Westerners use hard rock maple as their best, and a hard surface is all right for cutting cheese or cooked ham, and has the advantage of being easy to keep clean. But, the hard surface dulls the cutting blade of a sharp knife. Being hard, the grains are finer and smoother, which means less friction. But the Chinese require a certain amount of friction so that the meat being prepared will hold better on the block while executing a fine cutting.

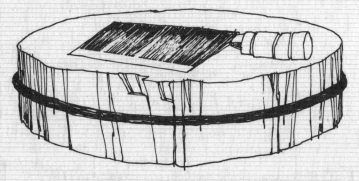

A manufacturer of Chinese chopping blocks never hires a designer with college degrees. Size is determined by diameter; thickness by common sense. Too thick is too heavy for handling, too thin may break. No instructions are furnished about how to use it and maintain its shape. Everybody knows to use one side for ordinary jobs, the other side for rough jobs or materials with smells which might penetrate into the wood grain. You must turn the block occasionally to maintain a flat surface. Never keep it under the sun as it may shrink; never keep it in water as it may swell. Nevertheless, a problem with shrinking or swelling may occur. If it does, you can correct it by simply reversing the procedure - if the chopping block shrinks, immerse it in water, if it swells - expose it to the sun.

Don't you agree that the Chinese chopping block deserves a special mention?

Don't be disappointed if you don't have a Chinese chopping block, for only certain kinds of dishes need professional cutting, for which a good block is essential.

If your cutting board has a very slippy surface, keep it aside for your cheese and ham.

A piece of plywood will do. The only thing to remember is what I mentioned in the beginning of this text; don't chop on it. A thicker one is better as a thin one might curl, seal the edge of the board with something waterproof.

KNIVES

When Chinese comment that someone knows little things about everything without any specialty, they say, "He has many knives; none is sharp." Several sharp knives are enough.

A professional Chinese cook will have: One cleaver, thin blade, for meat slicing or vegetable cutting; one medium heavy cleaver with a slightly curled cutting edge, for trimming raw meat such as pork legs, chicken, etc. If he does many jobs in minced meat, he has another pair of medium sized cleavers. (For a Chinese gourmet cook to use ground meat from a butcher is unthinkable.)

"HE DOESN'T KNOW HOW TO HOLD A KNIFE!"

"He doesn't know how to hold a knife" is a Chinese phrase indicating someone's lack of cooking ability. The important word is "hold" because, before you can use a knife, you must be able to hold it properly. And, if HE does not know how to HOLD a knife, then he is off to a very bad start indeed.

The cutting in Chinese cooking is very important, and unfortunately puts most people at a disadvantage when trying to cook. I am referring to family cooks, for in a typical Chinese restaurant, (with the exception of overseas Chinese restaurants) the Chief Cook only cooks, while the Chief Cutter (the real name for this job is the Chief Board, which means the one who is in charge of the cutting board) does all the cutting jobs. The cutter is the first one to receive an order. He picks the right ingredients, cuts them accordingly, and then hands them to the Chief Cook, who then cooks the dish. It is regrettable that many overseas Chinese restaurants do not follow the traditional kitchen system. It is the actual cutting which is a big part of the secret of making a delicious dish.

In one famous cookbook, a photo showed the au-

thor putting her first finger on top of the edge of the knife, which most people do. This is incorrect. Another famous gentleman, whose showmanship I very much admire (but only his showmanship), has a TV cooking show. He held the long blade knife as if holding a roman sword, and cut a whole chicken in half with one blow. He started the movement almost two feet above the chopping block, very swiftly and with a lot of force, and with his arm stuck straight out. As he stepped aside, the chopping block was almost a yard away! This is a dangerous way to cut a chicken, not to mention that you could have the cut you wanted only when your luck was with you.

Once a young Chinese girl was invited to stay with my daughter while I was absent. This lovely young girl did some cooking. During the preparation of the meal, she said, "Oh! How nice to use your knives, all of them

9

are so sharp." I felt very flattered for a dull knife is almost useless and I am proud of keeping my knives sharp at all times.

To keep a knife sharp you need a honing stone, a fine grain is good. A coarse grain on the other side is useful but not essential. Usually we are supposed to use only the fine grain stone to keep knives sharp.

To avoid being accidentally hurt, you can place the stone on the edge of a sink. If your sink has nothing to hold the stone in position, use a piece of wet cloth, or paper towel folded as a cushion. This will give you the friction needed to hold the stone in place.

CUTTING

The fundamental rule in cutting is to match the principal in shape and size to the complement, i.e. when you dice the meat, dice the complement too, etc. This will harmonize their appearance, and will equalize the cooking time for each.

Each piece of meat should be approximately the same size, and the thickness should be uniform throughout.

10

BEEF

1. Cut steak with grain into strips about 1 1/2 inches wide.

2. For slices, cut each strip across the grain into 1/8 inch slices.

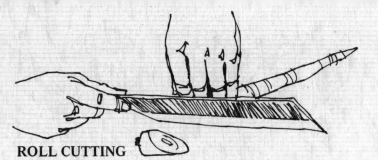

ROLL CUTTING

1. Make a diagonal cut straight down, roll carrot (turnip, potato, etc.) a quarter turn, slice again.

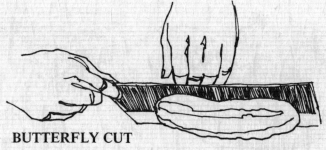

BUTTERFLY CUT

1. Cut cucumber in half, turn first half down.

2. Repeat until all of the carrot is used.

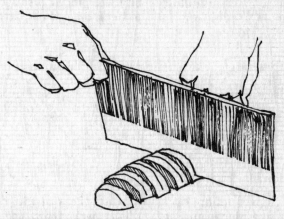

2. Make a cut most of the way through, move blade over and cut all the way through. Repeat on the rest of the cucumber.

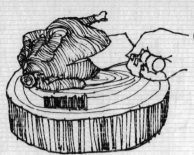

1. Cut off neck and cut into 4 - 5 pieces. Place in middle of platter. Cut chicken in half from tail to neck.

2. Cut wings off, cut into bite size pieces, arrange next to neck on end of platter.

3. Cut off leg and thigh section.

4. Cut back and breast sections apart.

5. With cleaver, chop back into bite size pieces and arrange so the meaty part (not boney part) is on outside of neck and wings.

6. Cut the outside of the thigh away from the bone by slicing down the bone. Cut into bite size pieces and place on outside of platter (opposite end from wings).

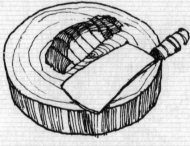

7. Slice breasts into bite size pieces and arrange over top of neck and back pieces.

8. When all is in place, it resembles a chicken again.

12

TERMS USED IN THE CHINESE MENU

The Chinese language uses only one simple syllable for each word or character and has no obligation to use all the time articles, prepositions, pronouns, etc. It is enough for the Chinese to express almost everything with only four words. But to translate Chinese to English and get the right meaning without a lot of words is difficult if grammatical rules are to be followed.

The English translation of Chinese menus are all different in the world. You just cannot standardize them partly for the reason that it would be too clumsy and partly because of personal opinion and preference.

The names I have given the dishes try, as the Chinese do, to mention the principal and the complement ingredients, the cooking technique, and the character of the seasoning. I do not use the sound of the Chinese in English spelling as it is funny to be pronounced by non-Chinese. The Chinese put the name of the complement first and the name of the principal last. It seems to me it sounds better for English speaking people if I put them in reversed order, as I did in this book.

Most dishes are normally salty which was understood, therefore, the salty taste was never mentioned.

When salted is mentioned it means "corned" in English.

Many dishes with a special cooking technique use a special kind of seasoning. This is understood and never mentioned in the Chinese menu but I mention the special seasoning in the name to help you get accustomed to remembering them.

CHINESE-FRYING

I came to the United States in January of 1969 after having spent the last sixteen years in South America, where I did not have an opportunity to read an English cookbook about Chinese cooking. I have intended to write such a cookbook for a long time as unless Chinese cooking is properly introduced, it cannot be properly appreciated.

There are more than 30 different cooking terms in Chinese cooking and one of the most difficult to understand is Chinese-frying. Every Chinese restaurant in the world prints on their menus the word "fried". People who have never had a chance to try Chinese food may misinterpret the simple word "fried". The Chinese menu lists fried rice, fried noodles, fried prawns and fried

13

chicken. In South America the word for fried is "frito" which means deep-fried. Chinese-frying is nothing at all like deep-frying.

I have now had a chance to read some Chinese cookbooks written in English by American Chinese, overseas Chinese, and even by Europeans. The Chinese cooking term which in English I call Chinese-frying is clumsy translated as "stir-frying", "agitate-frying", or even "brown and sauce". None of these terms indicate the cooking method very clearly.

Chinese-frying is the most typically Chinese way of cooking and different from the cooking of any other nation. However, I cannot give you a definition for all those dishes which bear the name of Chinese-fried, as a slightly different touch and treatment would be applied in each case. I will try to explain the technique in general and list some rules.

The wok is most ideal for this cooking technique and a skillet is the second choice. A flat bottom skillet will be fine for an electric range.

Strictly speaking, in a Chinese-fried dish, you should use just enough oil as you would for scrambled eggs. The dish should be on the dry side as in what they call a "fried rice" or "fried noodle" dish. Generally, a meat dish with vegetables as a complement in Chinese-frying will not use any water or broth. But sometimes a small amount of broth will be added with a small quantity of starch to bind the seasoning with the foods. If too much sauce is left after the foods are consumed, the Chinese will consider the dish incorrectly prepared. Never use a lid or cover while Chinese-frying or it will be quick-stewing or just simple cooking. The main purpose of Chinese-frying is to evaporate the moisture of the foods. If moisture is trapped by a lid or cover, the vegetables will lose their color and crispness and the meat will pass its point of tenderness.

Many dishes can be Chinese-fried within two minutes but three minutes are normally needed. When a Chinese-fried dish takes more than five minutes to cook, as many times happens in restaurants for a big order of twenty portions or so, you can be sure that the result is not satisfactory. You will notice after you have had some really good Chinese-fried dishes that a longer cooking time took away what the Chinese refer to as "wok-air" which is something that you cannot see but can certainly sense. I can hardly find the right word in English. Maybe the word "spirit" or "Spirit of a Dish" will give you some idea.

STEPS IN CHINESE-FRYING

1 - Wok must be very dry and clean. If not it will burn before coming to the right high temperature.

2 - In all Chinese dishes there are two basic parts; the principal and the complement. The principal is the meat, and the complement is usually a vegetable. In Chinese- frying you always cook the complement first.

3 - Calculate the amount of oil you will need to cook the complement (1 tablespoon is usually enough for a small portion). Preheat wok to a very high temperature, put oil in wok and then add complement immediately. This is very important, do not heat the oil in the wok before adding your complement otherwise the food will stick to the wok. The term used for this by professional cooks is "hot wok—cold oil".

4 - When the complement is almost 3/4 done, take it out, set aside, and keep it warm.

5 - Clean the wok with a paper towel, reheat to a very high temperature again and add about 3 tablespoons of oil to cook the principal.

6 - Note: Only 1/2 of the seasonings will be added to the marinade — the other 1/2 will be added when the principal and complement are combined. In this way, the seasonings will be well blended.

7 - When the principal is about 3/4 done, add the complement and remaining seasonings. Never add your seasonings before this time or the food will become soggy - except in cooking tough vegetables such as cabbage or green pepper. In that case, add a very small pinch of salt only when first cooking them.

8 - A very short period of time (about 2 - 3 minutes) is all that is needed for a good Chinese-fry. You will not have time to measure all the seasonings when you want to add them. Therefore, it is very important that you have them all ready beforehand. Use five or six very small containers (small saucers, pieces of paper, etc.), measure out the seasonings you will use, and place them on these containers before you start to cook anything. Place them within easy reach in the order in which you will use them.

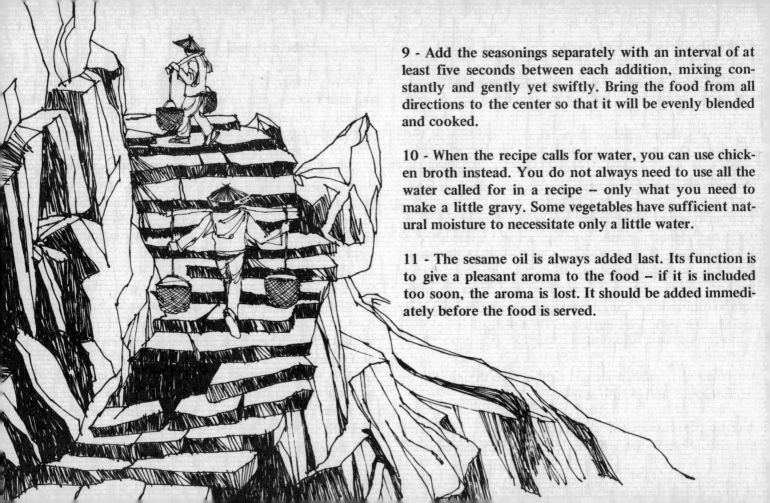

9 - Add the seasonings separately with an interval of at least five seconds between each addition, mixing constantly and gently yet swiftly. Bring the food from all directions to the center so that it will be evenly blended and cooked.

10 - When the recipe calls for water, you can use chicken broth instead. You do not always need to use all the water called for in a recipe -- only what you need to make a little gravy. Some vegetables have sufficient natural moisture to necessitate only a little water.

11 - The sesame oil is always added last. Its function is to give a pleasant aroma to the food — if it is included too soon, the aroma is lost. It should be added immediately before the food is served.

CHINESE-FRYING WITH SEASONED OIL

Soy bean paste is made from fermented soy beans. It has a strong flavor, and to a reader who has never had a chance to taste this paste, it is easily described as the smell of concentrated soy sauce with a dark brown color, packed in a can or jar as a coffee colored paste. If you like the taste of soy sauce, you will mostly also like the soy bean paste. A little bit of garlic combines well with the soy bean paste - it blends to make a warmer flavor. When soy bean paste is used, salt is no longer needed in the seasoning. Even soy sauce should be used very sparingly as the paste by itself is very salty. For this reason, more than the usual amount of sugar is used to compensate for the saltiness. Sesame oil can also be used more heavily than usual with soy bean paste. A typical use for the paste is with simple cooked noodles, drained, garnished with diced pork or other meats or vegetables, and Chinese-fried with soy bean paste seasoned oil.

If you read Chinese, or if your friends read Chinese, you may agree on which is the original Chinese word that I have translated as "Chinese-fry." But I am quite sure that it will be a puzzle for you to guess the original

Chinese word for "Chinese-frying with seasoned oil." In Chinese, it is a simple term meaning "exploring." This word was used for this cooking operation - in which the temperature is always high and the moisture is to be extracted in a jiffy, very much like the Chinese-fry. I think the name "Chinese-frying with seasoned oil" is quite correct as the operation is quite similar to Chinese-frying, except paste, garlic, green onion or even plain salt is used first to season the oil. Another difference is that in frying with seasoned oil mostly only meats are used and no water or broth will be added as in Chinese-frying. No starch will be used for thickening. On a Chinese menu, there is no difficulty in stating the seasoning followed by the Chinese word for "exploring". To make this practical in English, I modify the term i.e. "garlic-frying" means a dish Chinese-fried with garlic seasoned oil.

17

DOUBLE-FRYING

The original Chinese term for this cooking system means "returned-to-fry." It tells that the food has been fried, kept aside, and returned to the frying operation again. To make it simple, let's call it "double-frying." Certain rules should be observed:

The first frying should be done to the exact point of doneness. Do not try to under-fry, especially meats fried with a batter. Use not too high a temperature. Oil should always be sufficient in depth. If you have to minimize the oil being used, use a small pot and fry in small numbers.

During the second frying, use a high temperature, as this frying is to re-heat or re-crisp the fried food. If you have fried the food to the right point the first time, the second time you may judge your frying only by its color. If a desirable color has been reached, take the food out. The interval between the first and second frying should be long enough for the food to cool down. If you are in a hurry, five or ten minutes is enough. You may extend the time up to ten hours as long as the food is not refrigerated.

Double-frying is very useful for a big party, for al-though it increases your labor, it saves the last moment cooking time. Besides a double-frying is always better in certain dishes.

I mentioned before that by adopting Chinese cooking techniques you may improve your own cooking - try French-fried potatoes with a double-frying.

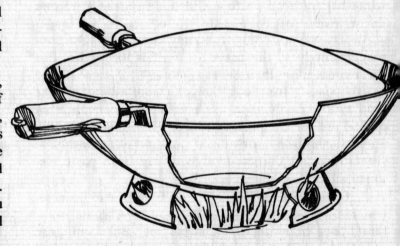

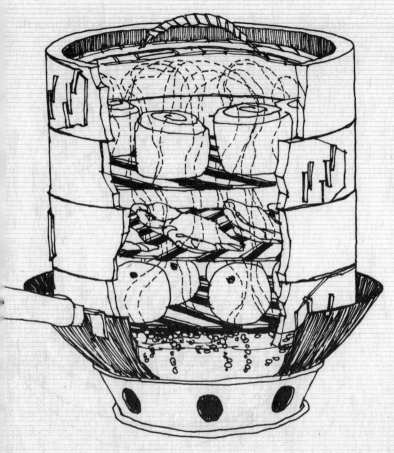

TRADITIONAL STEAMING

The lack of large quantities of easily obtained cooking fuels has caused the Chinese to become very economical in their cooking methods.

As already mentioned, the sloping sides of the wok pan tend to seal in the heat of the clay fire pot on which it is traditionally used. Little of the heat potential is lost in comparison to the "western" style flat bottom pan. Also, the high heat or temperature used to quickly cook the foods saves fuel as well as preserving flavor and food value.

However, there are some foods that require a longer, gentler, and more even cooking process. Either by choice or by the nature of the foods themselves, cooking with steam, or "steaming" is one of these.

Since most families already used the wok pan, it was only natural to adopt it for this task. The very things that make the wok good for "Chinese-frying" help make it an efficient steaming apparatus. By placing a small amount of water in the bottom of the pan, the direct heat of a very few briquets bring it quickly to a boil. If food is placed in the path of the rising steam, it will be cooked. Since the actual surface area of the water is

19

small, some method of capturing and using the full heat potential is needed. A series of circular, stackable, interlocking bamboo trays is placed in the wok pan to do this. These trays rest about half way down the sides of the pan, and tend to seal in the rising steam. They have slotted bottoms so that the steam may rise from the bottom to the top, cooking the various contents of each tray evenly. The amount of fuel necessary is the same whether one tray or six is used. No potential heat is wasted, and the water may be replenished at any time by pouring it down the inside face of the wok. No opening of the steaming trays is needed as with western style pans, so no precious heat escapes.

Another advantage of steaming in this way, is the ability to cook many different dishes at one time without mixing them together. If one type of food has a tendency to drip or flow, it may be placed on a lettuce leaf or small dish. One dish normally prepared in steaming trays is "deem sum." The section of deem sum snacks goes into more detail on this.

Try broccoli, cauliflower, or even pork chops in a Chinese steamer for an unusual and pleasing result.

Fish also lend themselves very readily to steaming since they cook quickly and must be treated gently. A western style dinner of steamed fish, broccoli, and potatoes may all be prepared on one stack of steaming trays with very little effort spent.

STEAMING

If you do not have a proper steamer, a big cooking pot will do the job.

You will steam the food in the same dish that you will serve it in. Put a plate in the bottom of the pot, and your dish to be steamed on top of the plate. Put enough water in the pot to cover the bottom, being sure not to use too much or it might spill over into the dish to be steamed. The plate is used as a support.

You will start to steam the food when the water reaches a fast boil. Five to fifteen minutes are needed for quick steaming. Thin sliced meat will require approximately five minutes, big chunks or a whole fish will require approximately fifteen.

Before you start to quick steam a dish, you must bring the food to room temperature otherwise condensation will occur and the food will become too juicy.

Slow steaming takes about forty minutes to an hour. When you use this method keep the water boiling at a low temperature and examine the pot often to make sure that the water doesn't evaporate away.

MARINATING

In professional cooking, each meat requires a different marinade, however, in general a dark meat marinade (used for pork, beef, chicken legs etc.) consists of:

1 1/2 T. dark soy sauce
1 T. wine (white, dry - never red or sweet)
1 T. cornstarch
1/2 tsp. sugar - to harmonize the taste, not to sweeten
1/8 tsp. pepper (optional)

A white meat marinade (used for chicken breast, prawns, fillet of fish, etc.) consists of:

1 tsp. salt (no soy sauce)
1 T. wine (same kind as for dark meat marinade)
1 T. cornstarch
1 egg white, unbeaten

The above measurements are calculated for 8 oz. of meat - one portion serving.

A good marinade requires at least 10 - 15 minutes at room temperature. If you refrigerate the marinade, always bring it to room temperature before using.

CONDENSING AND THICKENING

In Chinese cooking, cornstarch is the only thing used to thicken. You may substitute tapioca flour if desired, however, this is thicker than cornstarch and you will need less.

Dissolve one part cornstarch with three parts water and mix well before you add to the liquid to make gravy. Add slowly, stirring constantly to prevent lumping.

When the desired consistency is reached, serve immediately - do not overcook.

PORTION AND SERVING

Now we come to the recipes. Portion and serving are determined by personal preference to a great degree. There may be so much difference of opinion as to what makes a good sized "portion" to let us think others are abnormal - if not crazy! For instance, ten pieces of the Northern Chinese Stuffed Dumpling is usually calculated as a correct size portion. Some ladies can eat that much, many men eat only half a dozen, while some of my friends can eat as many as 50 or 60. Once we had a bet with a friend to eat a hundred. He lost the bet, but you can imagine how many he ate within a reasonable time of thirty minutes or so!

Even restaurants have no standard to determine the size of a portion for a single dish. In China, a single dish is normally consumed with two or three bowls of rice. At a party, the rice will be expected to be at a minimum, therefore the dishes should be increased to balance the total amount of food. The volume of a single dish should be enough to fill up an ordinary plate. This volume will be accurate up to eight servings if you prepare up to eight different dishes for a dinner. You might like to cook a smaller number of dishes - each having a

larger amount of food than is normal.

As the Chinese dinner is very versatile, you won't face the problem of five beef steaks for six guests. The actual volume of food might run short or over, but by applying some techniques of Chinese cooking the success of your dinner will be assured.

In this book, the portion is normally based on a plateful of food, as is generally taken at a buffet or luncheon. The plate is a standard size of 12 inches in diameter. The food will be piled up about 2 inches high on the plate. This is a regular Chinese standard portion as served in restaurants. In practice, you may order a double (called medium size plate), and a triple portion (called big plate).

A standard portion is supposed normally to be consumed by only one person, therefore a dinner party of various dishes would be calculated according to the number of varieties, then adjusted to the size of the dish. For example:

A dinner for six people would be calculated like this:

4 Variety dinner:

2 dishes of double portion	$2 \times 2 = 4$
2 dishes of standard portion	$2 \times 1 = 2$
	6
3 double portions or	$3 \times 2 = 6$
1 triple portion (e.g. a whole duck)	$1 \times 3 = 3$
1 double portion	$1 \times 2 = 2$
1 standard portion	$1 \times 1 = 1$
	6

In Chinese cooking, the problem with number of servings is very flexible. A chicken or duck is usually cut into about 40 pieces (bite size), to make any number of servings possible.

SALT

You may know many things about salt - you may even know that it is related to the word "salary", for in ancient Roman times, wages were paid in salt.

There is one story which I like very much about salt:

Once upon a time there was a king who had three daughters. One day the king asked each of his daughters how much they loved their father. The first mentioned gold and rare perfumes; the second mentioned diamonds, but the third said "Oh papa, you are my salt!" The king was very angry as he thought that salt was not very valuable and so he exiled his third daughter from his kingdom. Time passed and the third daughter was married to a prince. One day the prince had a party and invited the king as the guest of honor. During a banquet of many apparently delicious foods, the third daughter hid herself in the kitchen and ordered all the dishes to be prepared without salt. Upon tasting, the king suddenly cried out and remembered his third daughter for he realized that foods without salt make life unbearable.

Almost all dishes need salt and the taste of saltiness is most appreciated by all of us but besides this salt has many other utilities in the kitchen.

The old time Chinese cooks, without any formal knowledge of chemistry, knew that when their fire (they were cooking with firewood or charcoal) was not strong enough for their demand to just put some salt into the burning fire and immediately the fire goes – just enough to finish the dish.

A pinch of salt added in the oil before you cook any kind of vegetable will shorten the time of cooking and bring out the water content of vegetables right away to prevent a burn.

Many vegetables are salad fresh tossed -- in Chinese cooking called cool-mixed. If all vegetables are salted lightly a half hour before serving time it will squeeze out the water and leave space for the seasonings to be soaked in later on and most vegetables will be crispy -- except lettuce.

Salt also acts as an astringent. If a fresh fish is salted in the morning and prepared in the evening, the meat will be much firmer.

MSG (MONOSODIUM GLUTAMATE)

It was stated in one of the Chinese cookbooks that MSG was invented in Japan in 1908, and that in 1921 a Chinese scientist named Poo-Niew Wu developed a process for extracting MSG from wheat protein. It happens that I worked under the supervision of Dr. D. Y. Chow in the National Dyes Company in Hong Kong and I know that Dr. Chow, a famous chemist of the Nanking University and owner of the National Dyes Company, was the man who discovered the process of extracting MSG. I mention Dr. Chow here in remembrance of his valuable teaching.

People sometimes think that if a little bit is good, then a lot must be better. A make-up technician in Hollywood once mentioned this about some ladies' use of rouge. With MSG, cooks are no exception. Everybody uses it to make food instantly delicious, while many cooking arts are overlooked. Here are some essential things to be remembered about MSG:

Do not use it unnecessarily as the natural deliciousness of the food is enough.

MSG works proportionally with the amount of salt used, by itself MSG adds little to the food. To prove this, try to mix MSG with plain water. It is not delicious at all, which is one more reason why good cooking depends on seasoning and not just MSG. The amount of MSG used should be about 2 to 5% of the salt used. Many cooks use far too much. No wonder you feel thirsty after such a dinner. A small amount of MSG will not be harmful. Anything, of course, used to excess can be harmful, even vitamins.

SUGAR

Almost every dish can take a little bit of sugar, not for sweetness, but for a harmonizing effect. If after adding sugar, the sweetness is not noticeable, then you have probably attained the right effect. South Americans are shocked to learn that Chinese cooking uses sugar in most dishes. They think salt and sugar are unrelated but at the same time they not only use a pinch of salt in a sweet cake but eat bananas with seasoned rice.

The word "hot" in English has two meanings: it can mean either a high temperature or a hot flavor. There is a favorable soup in Sze-chuen cooking which is called Hot Sour Soup.

No soup will need sugar and most Chinese cooks know this. Many times the Hot Sour Soup has been badly seasoned because the cook remembered only the rule "no sugar in soup" but forgot the rule "sugar follows vinegar". People unaccustomed to this soup might be shocked at a soup "hot" and "sour"! But if rightly seasoned, the soup is very appetizing.

Sugar is always used in any dish which calls for vinegar. This creates the "sweet and sour" effect.

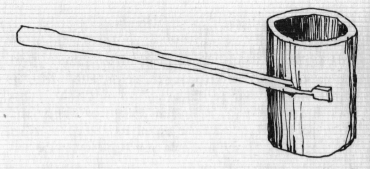

SUGAR-COLOR

In Chinese cooking, burnt sugar is used as coloring in many dishes, especially stews, when the dark color of the soy sauce is not enough to produce the color desired. If you use too much soy sauce to obtain the dark color, the dish will be too salty. To prepare the sugar-color, do the following:

Heat 2 T. granulated sugar on high temperature (do not use a teflon pan) until sugar is melted. Turn heat to medium low, stir constantly, sugar will turn dark brown. Do not burn too long or it will have a bitter taste. Add 1 cup water. The burnt sugar will not be sweet and can be used in place of regular water.

SOY SAUCE

There are two principal kinds of soy sauce – light and dark. Aside from affecting the color of this dish, the dark one has a stronger flavor and sugar should almost always be used with it. It has been aged longer and heavy sugar color has been added to darken it. When dark soy sauce is not available, use light soy sauce and add sugar-color to darken it.

Light soy sauce has more of the aroma of soybeans. Kikkoman soy sauce is a light soy sauce and can be found on the shelf of most supermarkets.

The light soy sauce is best used in soups, with white meat, and in cold dishes. The dark soy sauce is best in Chinese-fried dishes and stews.

VINEGAR

It is interesting to note that in all parts of the world, people make chairs with four legs. We also have chairs with only one or three legs, but never with two or five legs. Maybe all people agreed that four legs are better for making a chair. So it is with vinegar, both Westerners and Chinese agree to use it especially for a fresh tossed salad which in Chinese is called "cool-mixed".

Vinegar can be used very well to get rid of undesirable smells, for example in fish dishes. It will also solidify the fat of meat and is good while stewing a fatty pork.

A very delicious dish can be made from fish's liver, but without the vinegar the oil of the fish liver will run and the fishy taste will be unpleasant.

As vinegar is added, it softens bones. This will be noted while stewing any kind of fish with a lot of tiny bones. The bones will be soft and edible.

Vinegar will lose its acid taste by a longer cooking time. If the acid is required vinegar may be added just before serving. Remember "sugar follows vinegar" but vinegar does not have to follow sugar. All men have two legs, but all with two legs are not men.

OIL

Chinese use the oils of peanuts, soy beans, vegetable seeds, cotton seeds, and sesame seeds, among various others. Only the lard of pork, chicken, and duck are used. If you see any Chinese recipe calling for butter you can be sure it is a new invention by someone.

Peanut oil is the best as it has less smell than the others. Sesame oil is different -- it is expected to retain its aroma. In the United States, be careful when buying oil and read the fine print on the label. You may find "cotton seed oil" under the name of vegetable oil. You may like the cotton seed oil but I reject it because of its smell.

Hot oil will burn you easily when your hands are dry. When doing a lot of deep-frying, try to rub your hands and arms with oil -- a thin coating will prevent you from burning yourself.

WINE AND SESAME OIL

Wine is used in Chinese cooking for many dishes, but only in a very small amount. Usually a milder rice wine is used but certain vegetable dishes call for a strong dry wine. Chinese use wine for its deodorizing effect. It is used often with seafood to cover up any unpleasant smells. Meats are also very good mixed with dry wine. A typical Chinese-fried dish always calls for a little bit of wine -- it blends a better flavor but never leaves a noticeably strong smell or taste of wine. Chinese also use wine to characterize certain dishes such as the Drunk Chicken. Red wine has a bitter taste and is not suitable in Chinese cooking, although it may be used in a stew. If you do not care for the rice wine, any dry white wine may be used.

Sesame oil is used mainly as a perfume. It goes well with almost any dish of meat. Sesame oil is seldom used with vegetable dishes except for complicated mixed vegetable dishes which have no characteristic smell. Cold dishes go well with sesame oil, but when used with cold dishes it should be used lavishly.

If you can understand that the sesame oil is used as a perfume, then you will understand that in Chinese cooking the sesame oil is never to be cooked as it will lose its aroma by evaporation. Especially in a Chinese-fried dish, the dish is supposed to be served as soon as the sesame oil is added.

As a perfume, Chinese cooks never pay attention to whether or not the sesame oil is well mixed with the whole batch of food. It is just like the way you use perfume – you never perfume yourself from head to toe. How much sesame oil should be used? A little only. You never bathe in perfume do you?

You can always use a few drops of sesame oil in any kind of soup which has soy sauce. Add just before serving or use as a garnish in the soup bowl. Clear white soup does not go well with sesame oil. In this case, pork or chicken's lard, which is also used as a perfume, is very much better. In certain dishes, such as stewed vegetables, lard will do a much better cooking job.

Open, open Sesame! Do you believe these magic words? I see no magic at all. Not only will Sesame open the door for you but a lot of other things as well. Sesame may even bring you a box of candy or a mink coat or a martini or your slippers, if you happen to have a husband or wife named Sesame.

But let us get back to sesame oil seriously. In many places around the world you cannot get sesame oil, and as it is essential to Chinese cooking, you can brown sesame seeds at a low heat until the characteristic aroma comes out. You will not have the equipment to make oil, therefore, add in peanut oil twice the amount of

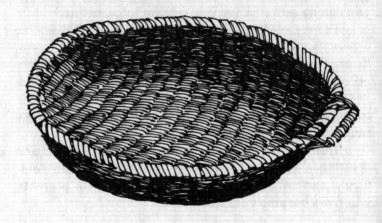

seeds. Heat to 280° for ten minutes. Cool. Use an electric blender at the highest rotation for 5 minutes. Set overnight. Filter the thin paste, you now have sesame oil and paste. The paste is very good for some cold dishes such as cool-mixed noodles.

BROTH AND STOCK

Do you know what the difference is between broth and stock? When it goes to the table, it is called broth. When it remains in the kitchen, it is just called stock. There are hundreds of recipes which talk about stock. There are also hundreds of "dos and don'ts" about the preparation of broth.

Prepared broth can be purchased cheaply in most supermarkets. I never have had a chance to observe the broth manufacturers preparing their products, but one thing I am quite sure of is that almost all of them use MSG.

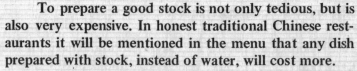

To prepare a good stock is not only tedious, but is also very expensive. In honest traditional Chinese restaurants it will be mentioned in the menu that any dish prepared with stock, instead of water, will cost more.

As I intend this to be a cookbook for you to be able to practice with, I will skip the traditional stock recipes and just indicate some "dos and don'ts" for your own homemade stock.

With the exception of fish, any kind of meat and bones are good for making stock. Parboil about 1/2 a minute, drain and rinse with cold tap water. Return to stock pot with cold water, bring to a boil slowly. When boiling point is reached, lower the heat and maintain the stock JUST under the boiling point. This can be achieved by cooking the stock without a lid. Continue cooking the stock for about an hour. Drain and filter the stock through a wet cloth or paper towel. Now you will have a clear stock and you may even have some of the drained meat left which you might enjoy seasoned with light soy sauce.

A stock should not be seasoned. It can be used with any dish in place of plain water. Rice cooked with stock is especially good and in this case seasoning would be required.

USE YOUR COMMON SENSE

There is a proverb that says: "If you believe books COMPLETELY, you are better off without books". This is very true, even if you follow something from a book, you still have to use your common sense. All the measurements in this book were carefully weighed in order to serve you as a guide -- only! They might not be good if the quantity is doubled or more. Many classic books say "adjust the seasonings" and that is your job. Among professional Chinese cooks, we change recipes only by cooking techniques, seasoning only mentioned as a little, a little more, and plentiful.

Remember that all seasonings of a different brand are not equal in strength. Soy sauce is no exception and even the plain refined sugar has such a big difference that it was unbelievable to me. I used to drink coffee once in a while during the last 16 years in South America. Of course I knew how much sugar I needed to mix in a cup of coffee. What a surprize to have to use more than double the amount to sweeten my coffee in the United States.

Meats of the same weight differ in moisture, the same is true of vegetables. One egg may be the same as one of your eggs for a fried egg. But one egg white to be used for marinating is quite different. The excess 1/2 tablespoon of egg white in a small quantity of meat might give you a problem.

Anyhow, use your common sense, learn by practice and correct with the next try. That is the universal way to learn almost everything, from archery to yachting.

SPICES AND CONDIMENTS

Spices are herbs and condiments are processed mixtures. In Chinese cooking, there are only several kinds of spices used:

Five fragrant spices
Tangerine peels
Flower pepper

The five fragrant spices are good for stewed meat and smoked fish. This spice is seldom used in soups or vegetables, with the exception of stewed pressed bean curd.

Tangerine peels are good for beef and duck soups or stewed beef and duck.

Flower pepper can be used in many dishes. It is an essential spice used in home-made pickles. The flower pepper has a characteristic aroma and a slightly bitter taste, but is not hot.

There are many other spices which may be used perhaps only once or twice a year. Since they are so seldom used, I have not included them in any recipes in this book, nor will I mention them here.

The primary condiments used are:

Soy bean paste
Black beans
Oyster sauce

Soy bean paste is a by-product of soy sauce. It has a stronger taste and smell than soy sauce and can be used with all kinds of meat.

Black beans are fermented and have a characteristic taste which blends very well with garlic and garlic should always be used with fermented black beans. To use, rinse roughly with water and soak or mash with garlic into a paste.

Oyster sauce is a condensed broth made from oysters and sometimes mixed with clams and seasoned with soy sauce. Usually it is to be used as a finishing touch and adds only a slightly different taste to a dish.

Shrimp paste is made of finely ground and cured shrimp. It has a strong seafood smell and is very appetizing. It is usually used with pork but sometimes with chicken and bean curd.

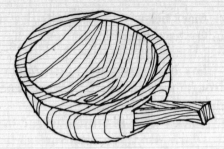

MEASUREMENTS

All the measurements in this book are based on weight (after trimming) for both meats and vegetables.

LET'S TAKE IT EASY!

I have heard the statements in a magazine "you should match meat to pot and what you want is a snug fit" and "to ensure a good fit, take your cooker to the market". No wonder so many housewives hate to cook! Imagine having to bring your pots to the market for shopping! The magazine showed many pots of different shapes for chicken, fish, stews, etc. -- all of them artfully designed. I hope to see what kind of shape would be a pot for lobster. This reminds me of an old proverb in Chinese about a man who cut his feet to suit the shoes!

Another book warned its readers on its first page that they could throw off the proportions entirely if they did not follow the measuring exactly as indicated. This lady author puzzled me as to whether she is teaching pastry making or plastic manufacturing. Do you still remember how to dilute sulfuric acid? Is it pour water into sulfuric acid or pour sulfuric acid into water? I believe that the procedures of each operation in chemistry should be followed faithfully. But the measurements for cooking should always leave a margin for under or over. If anyone wants to argue with me about this point, please answer why do all measurements come with round numbers such as 1/2, 1/4, etc? We never see such measurements as 4/5 or 7/8 of a cup or spoonful. Sifting flour changes the volume by 5 or 6%, but does not change the weight. Sifted flour may be better in puff cakes, but is certainly unnecessary for making noodles. Sifting flour for making noodles reminds me about a story of a man who opened a bigger hole in the door for his dog and a smaller one for his cat so they both could come in and go out as they pleased!

HOW MANY RECIPES DO YOU WANT TO COLLECT?

In one of my cooking classes, a lady told me that she has collected 165 cookbooks. If this lady had mastered only ONE recipe or cooking technique from each book, she would be an authority on cooking.

At one time I was the owner of the Universal Magic Circus in Shanghai. More than 60 artists worked there and many were the best in the entertainment field. All of my life I have been fond of magic. My sleight-of-hand is quite advanced and I would dare to challenge anyone. I once read in a famous classical magic book a story concerning a young man who met a well known magician and bragged that he knew over 300 tricks with playing cards. He asked the older man how many he knew. The older man was an authority in that field. He thought for awhile and then answered gently, "I should say I know about eight only." To know many tricks is one thing, to be master of them is another.

If the greater numbers means better, I could have written a cookbook with a number of recipes quite big enough to impress anyone. For instance, by simply using thirty cooking terms, times just ten principal meats, times twenty different varieties of complements would equal 6,000 different dishes. If you wish me to pass goal of a million, I could use the complements and the principals to make a combination. If you want still more than that, I could make each dish hot and cold, which would double the number of the total.

One book teaches 212 ways to prepare potatoes. One book teaches 365 ways of preparing hamburger. It tempts me to write a book about chicken - 1001 ways!

To gather all Chinese cooking techniques in one place would be a bore for you to read. Let's start one at a time with some recipes following for you to choose and try. For many reasons people are fond of reading cookbooks, but you certainly have to try and practice if you want to cook well.

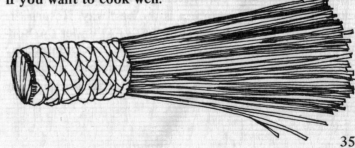

35

CHICKEN AND MUSHROOM SOUP

4 oz. chicken breast
1 oz. dried mushrooms
4 cups broth

Marinade for chicken:

1/2 tsp. salt
1 tsp. wine
1 tsp. cornstarch

Cut chicken and dried mushrooms into thin slices. Marinate chicken. Bring mushrooms to a boil using the broth. Keep the broth away from the burner and add the marinated chicken. Do not dump it in all at once or stir it otherwise the cornstarch will be rubbed off. Using chopsticks in this operation is the best way. Return the broth to medium heat and heat until just under the boiling point. The doneness of the chicken is determined by personal preference. You may serve it just under the boiling point - which makes it very tender, or you may simmer it for 1 more minute.

Variation: 1 oz. bamboo shoots, 1 oz. cooked ham, and 1/2 oz. Szechuan mustard pickles thinly sliced, may be added into the broth before the chicken slices.

PORK STRIPS SOUP

4 oz. pork
4 cups prepared broth

Marinade for pork:

1/2 T. light soy sauce
1/2 T. cornstarch

This soup is made exactly as Pork Slices Soup except that the pork is cut into strips rather than slices.

Variation: Cut 4 oz. bamboo shoots and 1 oz. cooked ham into strips and add just prior to pork.

PORK SLICES SOUP

4 oz. pork
4 cups prepared broth

Marinade for pork:

1/2 T. soy sauce
1/2 T. cornstarch

Sirloin is best for this recipe, however, if you can't find pork sirloin, use pork chops and trim off the bone.

Cut the pork into thin slices. Each person should get about 4 or 5 slices. Marinate pork. Bring prepared broth to a boil. Add sliced pork to broth. Simmer for 1 minute and serve.

Variations:

1) Add raw spinach (4oz. untrimmed) cut in approximately 2 inch sizes to soup just before addition of pork. Do not overcook or soup will turn black and bitter.

2) 4 oz. lettuce can be used in place of spinach. Cut lettuce into 2" x 1" pieces and add after pork.

BEEF AND LETTUCE SOUP

Lettuce is usually used only in fresh salads in Western style cooking. In Chinese cooking, however, it can be used very well in soup. The only thing to be remembered, is that lettuce should not be cooked. The best way to prepare lettuce soup seems to be as follows: Cut the lettuce into bite size pieces. When the soup is done, immerse the lettuce into the soup and serve immediately. If the timing is correct, the lettuce will maintain its crispness and its naturally sweet flavor, or otherwise the lettuce will become soggy, and the soup dark and bitter.

4 oz. beef
4 oz. lettuce
4 cups meat broth

Marinade for beef:

3/4 T. light soy sauce
1/2 tsp. sugar
1/4 tsp. wine
1/2 T. cornstarch

Bring the meat broth to a boil and add marinated beef gently. Simmer under boiling point for 1 minute, add cut lettuce and serve immediately.

BEEF AND WATERCRESS SOUP

There are two ways of preparing this soup.

1st way:	2nd way:
4 oz. beef	8 oz. beef
4 oz. watercress	8 oz. watercress

Using the first method, bring 4 cups of water to a boil with 1 T. oil and 1 tsp. salt added. Add watercress (trimmed and cut into 2" lengths). Bring to a boil again. Boil for 2 minutes, lower the heat, add the marinated beef slices, and heat just to the boiling point. Do not disturb the meat as the cornstarch from the marinade might rub off. This soup is now ready to be served.

Using the second method, bring 8 cups of water to a boil, add the beef cut into cubes or slices, and the watercress. Bring to a boil again and simmer for at least 1 hour. Adjust your seasonings to the amount of broth remaining and serve.

The first method is a quick way to make soup. The beef is tender and the watercress is crispy and green. It is very good for the summertime.

The second method takes longer to prepare, but the soup has a stronger beefy taste. The watercress becomes soft and pale yellow in color and brings a different taste to the soup. This is delightful during the wintertime.

To serve this soup, you may also do the following: Drain out the vegetable and meat from the broth and serve them separately. One dish is the soup, and the other is the beef and watercress. Season the beef and watercress with 1 T. hot oil and 1 T. light soy sauce before serving.

Soup which is cooked by long simmering should never have the salt added at the beginning; season it to taste just before serving.

NOODLES IN SOUP

The soup used with noodles should be a broth. Cook the noodles in broth, drain, and put in a bowl. At the same time, prepare Chinese-fried dish, thicken it heavily, arrange cooked meat and vegetables on top of the noodles, pour the broth carefully in at the edge of the bowl until noodles are barely covered with broth. The careful pouring is for a neat appearance.

Some standard Chinese-fried dishes such as Pork Strips and Bamboo Shoots, Chinese-Fried Three Strips, etc. are good with noodles. Stewed meats can also be served -- such as beef, pork, or chicken.

Here are some hints for cooking noodles:

Use a larger quantity of water with 1 T. oil added.

Add the noodles only when the water is already boiling.

When the water comes to a boil again, cover the pot and simmer the noodles -- the length of time for the simmering depends on the type of noodles.

Stir the noodles, folding the upper layer down and bringing the lower layer to the top, at least once.

Drain the noodles, rinse with cold tap water until cool.

If the noodles are to be stored for later use, add in 1 T. oil per pound of noodles, mix well, and drain again until no more water drips out. Spread the noodles out on a tray, cover with cloth or a paper towel, and keep in the warmest part of the refrigerator.

Many Chinese prefer to pay a higher price and patiently await a fresh dressed chicken. In Chinatown in San Francisco, there are two dressed chicken shops nearby each other on the same block to serve them.

As far as I know, most animal meat, if it is too fresh, will not be suitable for cooking. This is especially true for pork and beef -- it takes a certain length of time for the protein to set.

Freshly dressed chicken fanciers say that it tastes better, that it has more of a chicken taste. I think that this must be because most fresh dressed chickens are hens, while most frozen chickens are young cocks. Frozen chicken comes with less lard than the fresh, and this lard adds to the taste. There are two more differences also; fresh dressed chicken liver is much better than the frozen liver, and also the fresh dressed chicken skin is firmly attached to the meat. This is very important for poaching or deep-frying — it adds a great deal to the appearance, as for Crispy Fried Chicken.

A well-prepared Peping Duck is always made from a fresh dressed duck. Please note that I mentioned the name as "Peping Duck" not "Peking Duck," because "Peping Duck" was born earlier. "Pe" means north, and "ping" means level, flat, smooth, or plain. "King" means capital. The name of the dish was once named "Peping" and was later changed to "Peking" as now the capital of the mainland is located in the former "Peping."

If I were a duck, I would complain. You may change your own name, but how could you change my name without my consent? I like to stick with the name as "Peping Duck."

Choosing a live chicken is not very easy. If you only know to feel its legs and thighs, then you will not do too well.

I know how to select watermelons well, but not chickens. I know that to determine whether the bones are hard or soft you should feel the end of the breastbone. The color and fullness of the feet tells the texture of the meat. The anus tells whether it is a young hen or old. Certain special colors on the feathers tell the color of the skin, white feathers are the worst.

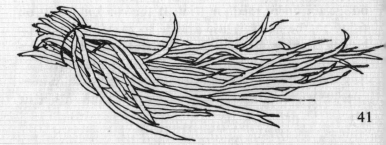

41

POACHED CHICKEN

In restaurants, poached chicken is usually presented as poached chicken in broth, because restaurants have the facility of plenty of broth. However, in family cooking you may poach chicken in plain water, after which you use the water to make soup or use it in cooking instead of water.

1 whole chicken
water - enough to cover chicken
1 tsp. cooking oil
1 tsp. sesame oil

Bring enough water to cover chicken to a boil. Immerse the chicken and then lift out again. Repeat this 3 times to bring the cavity to the same temperature as the rest of the chicken. Now bring the water or broth to a boil again under medium heat. If the chicken insists on rising to the surface, use a plate to cover it. When the boiling point is reached, turn the heat to the lowest setting, cover pot with a lid and cook for 30 minutes.

The timing is variable according to personal preference. For example, Cantonese like the chicken a little rare while the northern Chinese like it well cooked. Perhaps for Westerners I would suggest bringing the water to a boil again at the end of 30 minutes using medium to high heat. Then turn off the heat and keep the chicken in the stock for another 15 minutes. This chicken is to be served cold, although you may serve it warm.

After 5 minutes bring the chicken out and rinse it under tap water to get rid of only the grease on the skin. Do this with a cooking spoon inserted in the cavity (don't let the water get inside the cavity). Now brush with the cooking oil and sesame oil mixed together. This gives the meat a shiny appearance and keeps it moist.

Leave in the refrigerator overnight or for at least 1 hour (keeping away from the freezer compartment). Cut into 40 bite size pieces, serve with ginger and onion seasoning.

SAUCES FOR POACHED CHICKEN

Ginger and Green Onion Seasoning

Chop 3 stalks of green onion finely with 3 slices of ginger the size of a quarter. Mix together. Heat 2 T. oil until it smokes, then pour over mixture. Use as a dip for poached chicken when served cold.

White Sauce

Use chicken broth seasoned with salt and allow 1 tsp. light soy sauce per cup. Thicken the sauce, add several drops of sesame oil and serve with warm chicken.

Oyster Sauce

Use chicken broth seasoned with salt and allow 1 tsp. light soy sauce per cup with 1 tsp. sugar. Thicken, add sesame oil and serve with warm chicken. Pure oyster sauce may also be used - it comes in a bottle like ketchup.

SOY SAUCED CHICKEN (WHOLE)

1 whole chicken
4 T. dark soy sauce per pound of chicken
2 T. sugar per pound of chicken
2 stalks green onion, quartered
1 T. sesame oil

Wipe the chicken dry with a paper towel. Dilute soy sauce 1 to 1 with plain water, and add onion and sugar. Add the chicken. Using medium heat, cook the chicken with a cover. The heat should be strong enough to bring all the mixture to a boil, bubbling around and over the chicken, but not too strong as to evaporate the mixture too quickly. Turn the chicken every five minutes. When sauce is apparently too little in quantity, add no more than 2 T. water. (Wine may be used instead of water - the results are even better.) At the end of 30 minutes, pierce chicken leg with a toothpick, if no pinkish juice comes out the chicken is done.

Take chicken out and cool until you can handle it. Cut into 40 bite size pieces. (see cutting) Arrange on a plate. Remove onion from sauce, add 1 T. sesame oil, pour over chicken and serve.

DICED CHINESE-FRIED CHICKEN WITH BAMBOO SHOOTS

8 oz. chicken, diced
8 oz. canned bamboo shoots, diced
1 1/2 T. dark soy sauce
1 tsp. sugar
2 T. wine

Marinade for chicken:

1 1/2 dark soy sauce
1 tsp. sugar
1 T. wine
1 T. cornstarch

Chinese-fry the chicken until half done. Add the bamboo shoots and seasonings and continue cooking until the chicken is done.

Variation: Instead of bamboo shoots you may use any of the following:

green pepper - 8 oz.
red pepper - 8 oz.
celery - 8 oz.

Note: You can also combine any of the four, except do not use celery with bamboo shoots as they are very near to each other in color, and a contrast in colors is always more appealing. When a combination is used, the total weight should be 8 oz.

CRISPY FRIED CHICKEN

In this recipe you will use a poached chicken. When poaching the chicken first, however, the broth should be extremely salty - about 1 T. salt for every 2 cups of water.

water - to cover chicken
salt - 1 T. per 2 cups of water
1 T. vinegar
1 T. corn syrup

When the poaching is done, rinse the chicken and dry it with a paper towel. Make a mixture with the corn syrup and vinegar, and brush it all over the chicken. Hang the chicken in a cold windy place for at least a couple of hours or longer until the skin is quite dry. When you are ready to serve the chicken, heat a large amount of oil for deep frying. (The temperature should be about 340°.)

You don't need to immerse the chicken for a deep fry, but a depth of at least 1 1/2" is necessary. Lay the chicken on one side using a cooking spoon or ladle to pour the oil on top. Tilt your cooking wok or pan to help you in this operation. When a golden brown color is reached, turn the chicken over to the other side. Always pour the oil on parts that are lighter in color. When the chicken is good and brown all over, bring it out, and cool until you can handle it. (Professional cooks can handle any hot chicken as it comes out of the deep fryer therefore they can cut it right away and serve it immediately as too long of a delay will cool and soften the chicken's crispy skin.) Cut into bite size pieces. Garnish with parsley and lemon wedge - shrimp chips too, if available.

BUTTON

"Button" is a Chinese cooking term which means cooked in a bowl but served on a plate. It is used with a steaming technique and its purpose is to retain as much of the natural juices of the chicken, duck, or meat as possible.

Arrange the food, which was cut to size accordingly, neatly in a right size bowl suitable for steaming. This means that the bowl should be JUST big enough for the whole amount of the food - filled up to the rim. Meat in slices should be arranged piece by piece and side by side. Meat in slices with skin should be arranged as above but keep the skin side touching the bottom of the bowl.

Chicken or duck should first be cut and arranged on a plate in a heaping shape with the skin side on top. Now cover the whole batch with a bowl, forcing food neatly into the bowl. Now turn it upside down. The food is now in the bowl and ready for steaming.

You un-button when you want to serve a dish which has already been buttoned. It is just as when you serve a dessert which is in a mold. You put the plate on top and turn upside down. Food will now be on the plate ready for serving.

Before you un-button, be sure that there is no more juice in the bowl -- bring this juice out using a small saucer as a stopper. This juice should then be reheated and thickened to the consistency of cream sauce. Pour it on top of the food, which is already un-buttoned and piled up on a plate for serving.

STEAMED CHICKEN "BUTTONED"

1 whole chicken
1 cup or more broth
1 T. cornstarch per cup of broth

Steam the whole chicken for 5 minutes. Cool until you can handle. Button chicken in a bowl. (see buttoning) Thicken broth with cornstarch and pour into the bowl until the sauce level reaches 1/2" from the top layer of chicken. (As canned broth usually comes pre-seasoned, you will need no seasonings.)

Slow steam for 40 minutes. Drain out all sauce. (Cover meat with a saucer while draining out sauce to avoid disarranging the meat.) Now you need a second thickening to make the sauce denser. Un-button chicken on a plate and pour sauce on top.

STEAMED CHICKEN

12 oz. chicken (with bone and skin)

Marinade for chicken:

2 T. light soy sauce
1 tsp. sugar
1 T. cornstarch
1 tsp. sesame oil

Marinate chicken and cut into pieces of approximately 1" x 1". Arrange the pieces on a plate in a single layer and steam at medium-high heat for 10 minutes. (see steaming)

Variation:

1/2 oz. dried Lily Flowers
1/2 oz. Wood Fungus

Soak the above in water for about 15 minutes and drain. Then add in with chicken pieces. When Lily Flowers and Wood Fungus are used, increase salt by 1/4 tsp.

CHICKEN QUICK-STEWED WITH BAMBOO SHOOTS

12 oz. chicken
8 oz. bamboo shoots
3 1/3 T. dark soy sauce
2 tsp. sugar
2 T. wine
water - enough to barely cover ingredients

Cut chicken into pieces about 1" x 1". Cut bamboo shoots in rolling cut. Brown the chicken at a high temperature with 2 T. oil and 1/2 clove of garlic. Add 1 tsp. cooking wine until lightly browned. Add dark soy sauce, sugar, wine and water. Cook under high temperature with a lid. Stir every 5 minutes. (15 minutes is usually enough for this dish) By this time the sauce should be about 1/4 cup in quantity. Thicken it with 1 T. cornstarch, add several drops of sesame oil and serve.

CHICKEN WITH PORK STEWED

This recipe serves a double portion.

8 oz. pork
8 oz. chicken
1/2 clove garlic
1 small slice of ginger
4 T. dark soy sauce
3 tsp. sugar
3 T. wine
water - enough to barely cover ingredients

The boneless pork butt or leg is very good for this dish. Cut the pork and chicken into the same size pieces. (1" x 1") Using the garlic and ginger, brown pork and chicken at the same time with 2 T. cooking oil. Use medium-high heat until no more apparent juices come out.

If the cooking pot has something burned on the bottom, change to another pot. Simmer at low heat for about an hour. If you have an electric skillet, set it at 200°. Simmer covered until pork is tender. Before serving, adjust seasoning to the quantity of sauce remaining. Thicken with 1 tsp. cornstarch and serve.

48

Variation: 8 oz. bamboo shoots (rolling cut) may be used. Add them in during the last 15 minutes. Also add another 3/4 T. dark soy sauce.

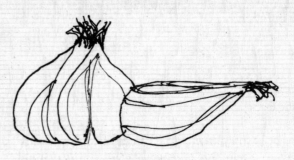

STEAMED CHICKEN

Salt a chicken heavily and leave in the refrigerator for two or three days but not in the coldest part, rinse quickly with tap water, wipe dry and steam for 20 minutes. This is a wonderful dish and can be served cold or hot. If rock salt is used, the meat will be firmer, and except for the breast the color will be pinkish as a cooked ham.

LOOO

There is an old tradition among Chinese restaurateurs; when a friend is opening up a new restaurant, the old restaurant owners would each send some of their own personally developed looo with their compliments so that the new restaurateur, now gathering up looos from friends would be able to have his loooed dishes up to standard.

Basically the looo is a method of storing, in liquid form, subtle spices and food essences. Each person uses a different amount or type of spice so that no two looos are quite the same. Also the food essences vary according to the age and frequency of use.

By sharing their looos with new people the older generation assures the continuence of this pleasant cooking art. Some owners as a matter of fact boast that their looos are hundreds of years old – which is possibly true. How nice are old time folks!

I have already mentioned that I don't like to use the English spelling for a Chinese word, but now I have a problem. If I don't use a simple word, it will take too many words to explain the meaning. Therefore, I use the word "looo". Yes, I use three o's. First, because that way it won't be confused with someone's name, and second because the three o's will remind you that this is a slow cooking technique. The ancient Chinese constructed words by the same kind of logic, for instance, there is one character or symbol for wood; two of these wood symbols are a forest, and three wood symbols are a jungle.

The looo, or as the Chinese call it "looo water", is made with traditional spices; soy sauce, rock sugar, wine, etc. It is not a stock or broth because you cannot use it for cooking any other dishes except those which are to be loooed. The looo water can also be used as a sauce to be served with loooed food. The looo may be kept indefinitely. Be sure to boil the looo each time before you looo the food. The longer in use, the better the taste of the looo.

Meats and boiled eggs can be loooed. Never use vegetables or fish and seafood. The meats are cooked in pure boiling water or parboiled for a short while, rinsed under running water, and then immersed in the looo. This is to clean and purify the meat so the looo will remain pure. Use a very low heat to keep the looo hot for an hour, or until the meat becomes tender, then leave the meat in the looo for another several hours or even overnight away from the heat source.

TO MAKE YOUR OWN LOOO

First, decide the quantity of looo you would like to make. Usually for a small family of two to four persons, one or two quarts are sufficient. Find a suitable container for keeping the looo. You may use the looo in a saucepot to looo your favorite foods, but you will have to store the looo in the refrigerator if you are not going to use it too often. It will keep several days in the refrigerator. If you don't have a suitable container, you may wrap it after it has chilled into a jelly. (If you have started with any meat that has skin in your loooing, the gelatine dissolved in the looo will make it into a jelly when cooled.) When putting looo away after use, be sure to strain out any excess particles to keep the looo pure.

There are two kinds of looo, a white and a dark. The dark is made with soy sauce. To begin, make the homemade stock for the looo using any chicken bones, pork bones, or even ham bones. Simmer the stock. Stock is a cooking term in the kitchen, it turns into broth when it is on the dining table. Strain the stock. To make the white looo, you will have to increase the amount of salt. Especially in the white looo some spice is very desirable, wine is also suitable. A typical spice for the white looo is Chinese Flower Pepper. It is reddish in color, the size of a pepper, but it opens as a little flower. It has a very good smell, but is not very hot. Six to ten grains of Flower Pepper are sufficient for almost two quarts of looo. If you would like a more Chinese taste, ask for ten cents worth of Five Fragrant Spices powder at a Chinese drug store, and add 1/4 tsp. for each quart. In case you are unable to find this spice, use a little bit of cinnamon and star anise seed. As a third choice, use bay leaves and cloves, and, for a fourth choice! Are you in the jungle? Ask Tarzan to spare you some spice he has!

To make the dark looo, mix half dark soy sauce, half light soy sauce, and dilute with homemade stock one to one. Season with salt to a quite salty taste. Add one tablespoon of dry cooking wine for each time you intend to use the looo. Rock sugar is best for the looo, if you can't find any, however, use ordinary sugar. The looo should taste salty but with a somewhat sweet taste also. Check the saltiness by tasting food after it has been loooed. If the food is not salty enough, increase the soy sauce and salt or vice versa. Pay attention to the cooking time in loooing also, as the longer in the looo, the saltier the food will be. Looos may be condensed by the stand-

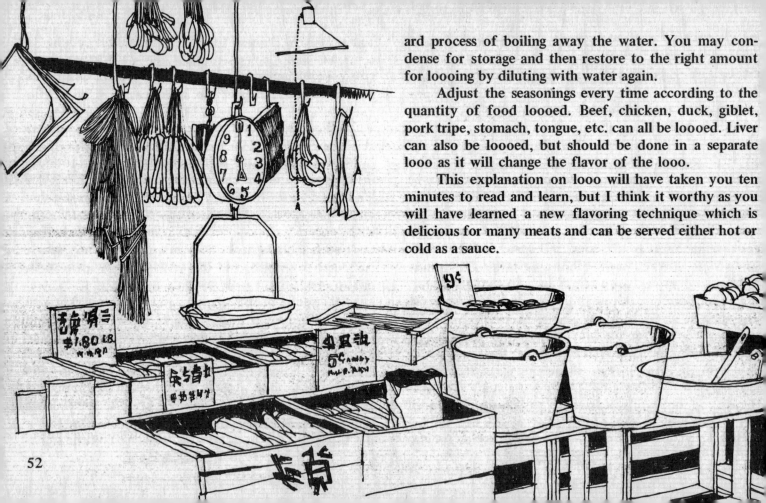

ard process of boiling away the water. You may condense for storage and then restore to the right amount for loooing by diluting with water again.

Adjust the seasonings every time according to the quantity of food loooed. Beef, chicken, duck, giblet, pork tripe, stomach, tongue, etc. can all be loooed. Liver can also be loooed, but should be done in a separate looo as it will change the flavor of the looo.

This explanation on looo will have taken you ten minutes to read and learn, but I think it worthy as you will have learned a new flavoring technique which is delicious for many meats and can be served either hot or cold as a sauce.

CHART OF COOKING TECHNIQUES ADAPTABLE WITH GENERAL PRINCIPLES
CHART OF PREPARING MENU FOR A DINNER PARTY OF VARIOUS DISHES

	Beef	Chicken	Duck	Fish	Pork	Prawn	Internal Parts*	Vegetables
Basing							x	x
Buttoning	x	x	x		x			
Chinese-frying	x	x	x		x	x	x	x
Circling		x	x		x			
Chinese-frying with seasoned oil	x	x	x	x	x	x	x	
Cool-mixing		x			x		x	x
Deep-frying	x	x	x	x	x	x	x	
Double-frying		x	x	x		x		
Loooing	x	x	x		x		x	
Shallow-frying	x-a			x	x-a	x		
Smoking		x	x	x	x			
Steaming	x	x	x	x	x			
Stewing	x	x	x	x	x			
Quick-stewing		x		x	x	x	x	x
Water-bathing	x	x	x		x		x	

*liver, kidneys, hearts, tripe, tongue, etc.

54

This chart serves as a general guide for choosing combinations of principals and cooking techniques; however, there are many exceptions to it, as your choice of complement may not be suitable for a certain cooking technique. (Principal refers to either meat or a simple vegetable dish, complement refers to a vegetable added into a meat dish.) To plan a dinner party of various dishes, try to pick no more than one x, either vertically or horizontally. (Occasionally 2 x's are acceptable.) For instance, Beef Chinese-fried, Chicken Poached, Duck Steamed, Prawns Quick-stewed, Fish Shallow-fried, etc. Also, visual aspects of the foods used should be considered, i.e. color combinations.

The Chinese never repeat in a single meal dishes with the same meat, same color, same cooking technique, or same taste.

Only the cooking terms that have been explained in this book are included in the chart. Each x should have at least one related recipe or variation of a recipe included in the book. If you cannot find it, return to the section that deals with that technique in detail, and follow those instructions.

x-a - Pork chops are the only cut of pork that can be shallow-fried in Chinese cooking because this technique might result in rare meat which is inadvisable. Medallions of beef is a modified Western dish. Therefore, neither of them have been selected for this book.

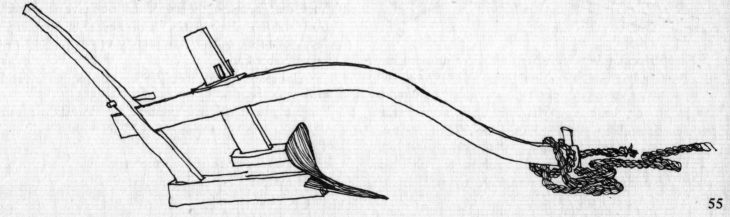

HOW TO JUDGE A CHINESE DISH

I presume that I know how Westerners judge a good dish by their own standards but I am not going to occupy the space of this little book with that discussion for you might know better than I do. If you agree that to know how to cook is not very easy, then to know how to judge a good dish is also not very simple.

I still remember the story about a man who lived by knowing how to choose and judge dishes for a group of wealthy Chinese gourmets! He was always invited by the group for the every-night-dinner at various restaurants in Shanghai — before World War II, of course. I think it was because he knew how to choose and judge a dish, although he did not know how to cook, that made the Chinese Chefs try so hard to meet his de-

mands and thus provide a better dinner for his employers.

Mandarin cooking is very advanced because of the kings who used to live in that part of China. They were served only the best by their cooks, who tried always to please them. In other provinces the Chinese cooks only tried to please their fellow folks' taste.

The following are points to be criticized in a Chinese dish, especially a Chinese-fried dish as it has more chances to go wrong.

Tastes should be harmonized and well blended.
Sauce should be at the right amount.

Dish should be evenly cooked. You will find many times that because the cook did not give the meats a good mixing during the Chinese-frying that several pieces of meat will be completely raw while the rest is correctly cooked.

Complement unwisely chosen, for example, fish with bean sprouts.

Judgment of time control. Serving should not be interrupted. No clumsiness should delay the final touches of serving.

Oiled incorrectly — either too much or too little oil.

56

Uniform cutting – certain standard sizes and shapes should be followed.

Proper arrangement in decorating and pleasing colors.

Quality of raw material -- although the cook does not produce the ham his choice makes him responsible.

If you can award a dish ten points it will be perfect which is impossible. Maybe for this reason we have only nine points.

WHEN THE RESULT IS NOT SATISFYING

I know nothing about how to spot the trouble on a TV, but the TV trouble shooting charts always tell me that "Your Local Station" is first to be blamed! I have no courage to blame you if anything goes wrong and you followed my cooking instructions. First, to describe in detail is still not enough to communicate the knack in cooking, and second, it is hard to follow a cookbook when nothing is the same in any two kitchens, from the material used to the equipment and heating conditions. You must use your common sense and not be afraid to try again. I even encourage you to use your judgment

and make some modifications to suit your own taste.

Let's return to the section on judging a Chinese dish. If the taste is not harmonious, use more salt and soy sauce or more sugar. If it is too strong, the second best way is to dilute the sauce and leave the excess sauce apart. The best way to correct is in your next try.

If there is no sharpness and contrast and if the dishes do not stand out, it is very simple -- you did not dare to season it "sharp and contrast". In a hot dish, chili, mustard, green onion, garlic, leeks, or spices are probably the ingredients that were not used enough.

If the dish is of a very ordinary flavor, it will probably be because the dish was cooked over too low a heat or not sufficient ginger, garlic, etc. was used. The just-before-serving touch of a few drops of wine and sesame oil is very important.

The right amount of sauce is very easily adjusted if you are not in a hurry. Always judge the right amount of water or broth to be added. Always thicken the sauce little by little, pausing to see the result. Stop when the sauce is almost at the right point as it will get thicker yet. Remember, it is easier to thicken than to dilute.

Cook evenly -- keep the Chinese-fry always in movement. It should be a movement like folding cream into a dessert, but quicker and from all directions to the center.

The complements in this book are well suited to the dish, but at times you may want to substitute. The serving will hardly ever be interrupted during a family cooking as may happen in a restaurant. An incorrect amount of oil can only happen in restaurants when the cooks do not want to lose points for "serving interrupted". They neither drain out the excess oil, nor add some more.

Amateur family cooks will be at a disadvantage in cutting uniformly. You might lose points in cutting a whole fried chicken into pieces as a professional does. He can handle a hot chicken without burning his hands and cut it into 48 pieces in less than two minutes, and by the time he finishes the last cutting, he will have the whole chicken correctly arranged and piled up on a plate. But don't mind this point, you may gain a point for paper-thin slicing. Meat frozen to just the right point can be cut paper thin while a professional cuts meat unfrozen, which takes a long time to practice.

You can almost always do better than a professional Chinese cook at decorating a dish in an eye-catching way. They probably learned this from non-Chinese cooking, perhaps from you!

A MODIFIED DUCK DISH

This is a famous dish in Sze-chuen cooking. The principal is a duck steamed until done, then deep-fried until crispy.

As deep-frying a whole duck in a family kitchen is a problem, I have tried a modification and it seems to me that in this way, the meat will retain more moisture.

Using a big pot, cover the duck with water, add salt (about 1/2 tsp. per cup of water), and simmer at a low heat until the meat is tender, about 1 to 1 1/2 hours. Take out duck and drain. Season with pepper and salt, inside the cavity and out. Brush the duck with oil and broil under a high temperature until brown all over. Turn the duck every 5 or 10 minutes and brush with oil if necessary. A coat of soy sauce mixed with oil may be used for the last coating to bring a quick brown color.

Serve the duck whole. Duck prepared in this manner is very easily carved on the table, using only chopsticks or a knife and fork.

You still have your broth left, which is ready to be served as it is, or you can also add:

Bean curd cut into cubes or thick slices, boil for 5 minutes in broth.

Turnips (rolling cut), stewed in broth for 30 minutes.

Spinach may be used, add into the broth and boil for 1 minute.

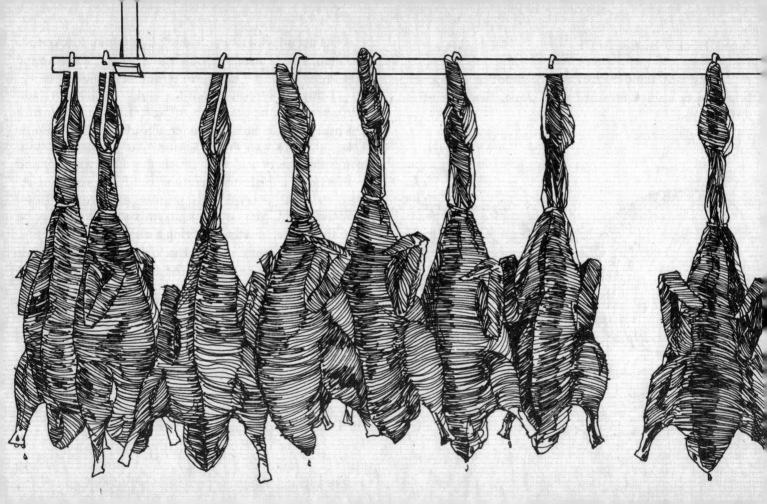

KING OF PORK CHOPS

Pork is greatly used in Shanghai cooking. Shanghai families seldom cook beef. One poor food vendor made a small fortune by deep-oil cooking pork chops and turning it into a big business. He was named afterwards the King of Pork Chops during the late 1930s.

He sold the pork chops as a lunch or as cooked food for people to take home. He sold nothing but pork chops in his place where not even the counter is impressive. I figured out that people bought pork chops from him, not because they could not do it in their own home kitchens, but mostly because the Chinese are very economical, and considering the small amount of profit made by the King of Pork Chops, it did not pay them to keep the large quantity of oil needed for this cooking system.

I do not feel ashamed to tell the readers that when I was a boy, although raised in a wealthy family, many times we bought hot boiling water from the nearby hot water vendor. To keep our coal burning stove going all day long is very costly for only several quarts of hot water which the vendor produced by burning firewood in big quantities.

When I see people throwing away good prepared and unconsumed food it disturbs me very much. We might save very little, but we consider saving anything as a virtue.

KING OF SHANGHAINESE PORK CHOPS

Use thin pork chops if possible.

Marinade for each pound of chops (3 to 4 chops):

    1 T. light soy sauce
    1 T. dark soy sauce
    1 t. sugar
    1 slice of ginger
    stalk of green onion

Marinate chops 10 to 15 minutes. Dry and deep-fry in medium hot oil (325°). Drain well. Sprinkle with five fragrant spice before serving.

PORK SLICES CHINESE-FRIED WITH CELERY

8 oz. pork
10 oz. celery
mushrooms - either 1 oz. dried or 4 oz. fresh
1 1/2 T. dark soy sauce
1 tsp. wine
1/2 tsp. sugar
1 tsp. cornstarch for thickening

Seasoning for mushrooms:

1 tsp. dark soy sauce
1/2 tsp. sugar

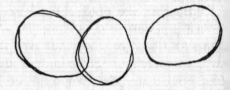

If dried mushrooms are available, use 2 or 3 pieces per portion. Soak mushrooms in water overnight, or for at least 15 minutes to soften. Cut in thin slices. Chinese-fry them first, adding seasonings for mushrooms. Add celery and 3 tablespoons of water and boil until all liquid is absorbed. Set aside. Proceed with Chinese-fry of pork.

Finishing touch: Thicken with cornstarch, add wine and sesame oil and serve.

STEAMED MINCED PORK WITH EGGS

8 oz. pork
2 eggs
1 T. light soy sauce
1/4 tsp. sugar
1/2 tsp. cooking oil
1/2 tsp. salt

Mince pork (see mincing), and season with light soy sauce and sugar. Beat 2 eggs with double the amount of water. (You can measure the water in the egg shells.) Add the cooking oil and salt. Blend the mixture with the pork. Proceed the steaming at a low temperature. (see steaming) Why at a low temperature? - A high temperature would cause the mixture to bubble.

Finishing touch: Pour 1/4 tsp. dark soy sauce on top and swirl around to coat top of the food.

PORK SLICES CHINESE-FRIED WITH CUCUMBER

8 oz. pork marinated
12 oz. cucumber (2 - 7" cucumbers trimmed)
1/2 T. dark soy sauce
1 tsp. sugar
1 tsp. salt

Marinade for pork: regular

Cut cucumber in double-butterfly cut and remove seeds. Be careful not to cut the slices too thin or they will become soggy. Cook the cucumber until 3/4 done with the above seasonings. Proceed with the regular Chinese-fry procedure with the marinated pork.

PORK SLICES CHINESE-FRIED WITH MUSTARD GREENS

Mustard greens are abundant in California and have a very pleasing aroma. Here is a good way to prepare them:

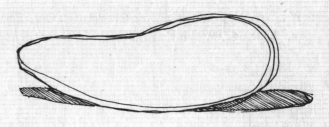

8 oz. pork
12 oz. mustard greens
2/3 T. light soy sauce
1 tsp. wine
2/3 tsp. sugar
1 tsp. cornstarch for thickening
1 tsp. salt

Marinade for pork: regular

Bring a large amount of water to a boil. Wash and slice mustard greens, then parboil. 1 minute is the maximum time for boiling. The parboiling should be done at the same time as you start to Chinese-fry the pork. This way, when your pork is almost half done, the mustard greens will be reaching the 1 minute limit. Drain the mustard greens immediately, add to the pork and finish the Chinese-fry.

PORK STRIPS QUICK-STEWED WITH CONDENSED SAUCE (ACCOMPANIED BY CHINESE CABBAGE)

8 oz. pork butt
20 oz. Chinese cabbage
3 T. dark soy sauce
1/2 tsp. salt
1 tsp. sugar
1 tsp. wine
1 tsp. cornstarch for thickening

Marinade for pork: regular

Cut pork and cabbage into strips of equal size. Marinate pork. Heat wok, add oil, and put in meat. When meat is 1/2 done, add Chinese cabbage. Add seasonings in the following order: soy sauce, salt, sugar, and wine. Add water to barely cover contents. Cover with lid, cook at high temperature for 5 minutes. Remove lid and stir -- repeat after 5 more minutes. The water content should now be reduced to 1/2 its original volume. Add cornstarch to condense sauce (see condensing and thickening).

This is a typical Shanghai dish.

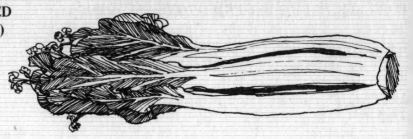

PORK STRIPS CHINESE-FRIED WITH CELERY

8 oz. pork
10 oz. celery
1 T. dark soy sauce
1 tsp. sugar
1 tsp. wine
1/2 tsp. salt
1 T. cornstarch for thickening

Marinade for pork: regular

Cut pork and celery into strips. Marinate pork. Follow procedure for Chinese-fry.

64

PORK STRIPS WITH TRANSPARENT VERMICELLI

Transparent vermicelli can be bought in dried form and is made from the starch of mung beans. It is also called Long Kow Bean Threads.

8 oz. pork
2 oz. transparent vermicelli
1 1/2 T. dark soy sauce

Marinade for pork:

1 1/2 T. dark soy sauce
1 T. wine
1 tsp. sugar

Soak the vermicelli in warm water for approximately 10 minutes. Cut pork into strips.

Bring vermicelli to a boil, then cover and set aside for 1/2 hour. Cut with scissors into 3" lengths and drain. Chinese-fry pork strips until half done, add drained vermicelli, cook at medium heat for 5 minutes. Add water or broth when vermicelli appears to be getting dry, continue adding water until vermicelli will absorb no more liquid.

Note: Did you notice that the pork in this dish is to be cooked about twice as long as usual? The texture of some meats is spoiled by a longer cooking time, but this is not true for the pork in this dish.

PORK STRIPS CHINESE-FRIED WITH BAMBOO SHOOTS

8 oz. pork
8 oz. bamboo shoots
1 1/2 T. dark soy sauce
1 tsp. sugar
1 tsp. wine
1/2 tsp. salt
1 T. cornstarch for thickening

Marinade for pork: regular

See section on bamboo shoots. Follow procedure for Chinese-fry.

BAMBOO SHOOTS

When a recipe calls for bamboo shoots, you should use canned, saltless, unseasoned bamboo shoots.

Cut and season according to recipe (i.e. dice, slice, etc.). Then simply add them with the meat as they are pre-cooked and require no other cooking.

Fresh bamboo shoots are not as plentiful in the United States as in China. The spring bamboo shoots are tender and stout. The summer bamboo is lean and thin and has a strong aroma of bamboo. The winter bamboo shoots, which must be dug out from the ground, are firm and delicious.

The spring bamboo is the first harvest. During the early part of spring the bamboo stays and grows underground only. After the first spring rains, the moisture gives the bamboo strength to suddenly sprout out of the ground with a noise like a small firecracker. It sometimes happens in a very short time of perhaps only several minutes or so. You will find that where a bamboo field was quiet and calm, suddenly you will hear all around you the noise of many small firecrackers and you will find hundreds of bamboo shoots now growing above ground. We use this phenomena as a standard adjective to describe a mode or trend which suddenly becomes popular. For instance, we never had mini-skirts before, and now suddenly we have many mini-skirts like the bamboo shoots after spring rain.

PORK STRIPS CHINESE-FRIED WITH TURNIPS

8 oz. pork
14 oz. turnips
1/2 T. dark soy sauce
1 tsp. salt
1/2 tsp. sugar

Marinade for pork: regular

Turnips need a little more time to be cooked than other vegetables, therefore, cook them until completely done. Add the seasonings when you are cooking the turnips. Procede with the Chinese-fry with the pork. When pork is completely done, add the turnips and mix well, thicken sauce and serve.

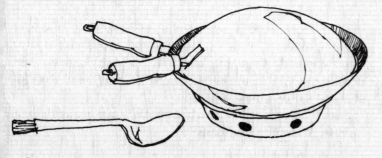

PORK STRIPS CHINESE-FRIED WITH RED PEPPER

Red pepper is only a green pepper that has been left in the ground to mature for a longer period of time. It has the same taste as the green pepper.

Chinese use red pepper in cooking hot dishes to give them the appearance of being spicy. To obtain the spicy taste, however, chile powder is added.

8 oz. pork
5 oz. red pepper
1/4 tsp. chile powder (or more to taste)
1/2 T. dark soy sauce
1 tsp. wine
1/2 tsp. sugar
1 tsp. cornstarch for thickening

Marinade for pork: regular

Cut pork and red pepper into strips. Pepper is trimmed and only the outside skin is used. (see trimming) Follow procedure for Chinese-fry.

CHINESE CABBAGE

There is a vegetable usually referred to as Chinese cabbage. It can be substituted for regular cabbage in any recipe (not vice versa, however), but certain care must be taken. Chinese cabbage has a naturally sweet taste, therefore, sugar should be used very sparingly. Chinese cabbage does not always have the same texture as regular cabbage – its consistency changes as you cook it (whereas regular cabbage stays the same). Therefore, be careful not to overcook it. When using Chinese cabbage in Chinese-frying, it is best to use only the white crisp part, the yellow part is unsuitable for a Chinese-fry. You can use the yellow part in vegetable soup. One dish using Chinese cabbage is with cream sauce or oyster sauce.

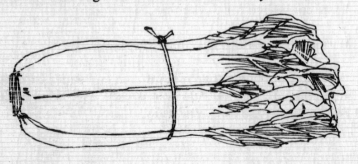

CHINESE CABBAGE WITH CREAM SAUCE

Cut Chinese cabbage into strips of 3/4" x 6". Lay in the bottom of a pot and cover with chicken broth. If canned salted chicken broth is used, no seasoning or extra water is needed. Simmer until very soft (about 30 minutes). When liquid is reduced to 1/2 its original volume, drain the vegetable and lay it on a plate. Add enough milk to the remaining broth to bring it up to its original volume of one can. Thicken with 2 T. cornstarch, 2 T. whipping cream, and 1 T. oil. Pour on top of vegetable and serve.

CHINESE CABBAGE WITH OYSTER SAUCE

Oyster sauce is prepared the same way as cream sauce except: Use water instead of milk, and oyster sauce instead of cream. Add 1 T. dark soy sauce when cooking vegetable in the beginning. Use saltless broth instead of salted chicken broth.
*Oyster sauce is a bottled, prepared sauce available in a Chinese store or supermarket.

PORK BALLS IN BROTH

8 oz. pork
1 qt. (4 cups) broth
Season to taste

Marinade for pork:

1 1/2 T. light soy sauce
1 T. cornstarch
2 T. water

Mince pork finely and marinate. Bring the prepared broth to a near boiling point. (see section on broth) Prepare meat balls (see picture) and dip the meat balls in broth. Bring the broth to a boiling point. Simmer for 2 minutes and serve.

STEAMED FIVE-FRAGRANT SPICES SEASONED PORK WITH BROKEN RICE

1 lb. pork
2 1/2 oz. rice
1/4 tsp. Five Fragrant Spices

Marinade for pork:

3 T. dark soy sauce
2 tsp. sugar
1 T. wine
1 tsp. salt

Marinate pork for 1/2 hour. Mix with Five Fragrant Spices. Brown raw rice over low or medium heat until brown. Break rice either in a blender at low speed or with a rolling pin. Rice should be coarsely broken. Add a considerable amount of water to broken rice and drain. Add 1/2 T. dark soy sauce. Coat marinated pork, piece by piece, with broken, moistened rice. Button (see buttoning) the pork in a bowl. Steam over low heat for 1 hour. Check at intervals of 20 minutes, if rice appears to be drying, add a small quantity of hot water. Unbutton on a plate and serve.

STEAMED MINCED PORK WITH SALTED EGGS

8 oz. pork
1 salted egg

Marinade for pork:

1 T. soy sauce
1/2 tsp. sugar
1 tsp. cornstarch
4 T. water

(See salted eggs) Mince pork and place on the bottom of a plate. Tap it slightly in the middle with the bottom of a spoon for centering the egg yolk. Break the salted egg on top of the meat. Steam slowly for 20 minutes.

HOMEMADE SALTED EGGS

Use a big open glass jar. Put eggs in jar carefully. Fill with tap water until eggs are well covered. Drain the water out – this is the amount you will need to make your salt solution. Boil this amount of water. Slowly add salt, spoonful by spoonful until the water cannot dissolve any more. Set salt solution aside to cook by itself. In the meantime, dry the eggs in the sunshine for 15 minutes. Arrange the eggs again inside the jar. Pour the cooled salt solution over to cover the eggs. Because of the density of the solution, the eggs will float. Leave for about 28 days in a cool place (do not refrigerate). Examine the eggs after about 21 days.

Because personal preference cannot be determined, boil one egg as usual (because the egg is salted it will require at least 15 minutes to become hard boiled). Now peel egg and taste to see if it is salted to your taste. You may stop the procedure now by bringing all the eggs out and storing in the refrigerator, or you may continue until 28 days. When a longer time is spent, usually the eggs become more salty and the yolk, by a chemical reaction, turns oily by itself and the color is more reddish than usual -- this gives a delightful appearance.

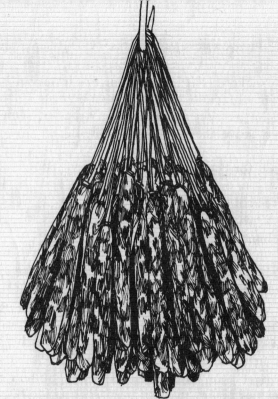

During the preparation of the eggs, be careful not to crack the shells as the eggs will become too salty. If correctly stored, the eggs will remain good for months.

71

ROAST PORK OR RIBS

Nowadays, roasting is no longer a restaurant's specialty as most families have their own oven.

A longer time in marinating is better, sometimes you may leave the meat in overnight.

Marinade for roast pork:

2 1/2 T. light soy sauce per 8 oz. of pork
1 1/2 T. wine
1 tsp. honey or corn syrup

Don't use dark soy sauce or sugar as these tend to burn before the pork is cooked.

When a dark color is desired, brush with a coat of soy sauce mixed with oil during the last 5 minutes. Trim the pork lengthwise rather than in a cube. 1 1/2" x 1 1/2" in thickness is good for roasting.

Forget your time-table that tells you how many minutes per pound of the meat. It is the thickness that determines the time needed, normally 20 to 30 minutes is enough. Check the doneness by cutting a slit in the meat to see, this is much easier and more accurate than using a thermometer.

When ribs are roasted, the shrinkage of the meat from the bones tells the doneness. Don't judge by the outside color - it isn't a reliable indication of doneness.

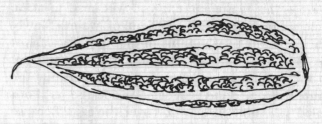

PORK CHOP SOUP STEAMED

1 chop per cup of water
1/2 tsp. wine

This is a very clear soup and you can make it effortlessly. The taste is pure and simple, and very appetizing.

Use one chop per cup of water, and add 1/2 tsp. wine. Arrange chops in a deep soup bowl or casserole. Steam at a low temperature for an hour. Add salt to taste before serving.

STEWED PORK IN PIECES

1 1/2 lb. pork butt
1/2 T. cooking oil
1/2 clove garlic
4 1/2 T. dark soy sauce
1 1/2 T. wine
5 T. sugar

Brown pork with oil and garlic. Keep browning until no more juices come out of meat. Add the soy sauce, wine, and sugar. Follow with 1 cup water. If the bottom of the pot is burned, change meat to a different pot. Simmer until done (approximately 1 hour). Thicken gravy with 1 tsp. cornstarch.

With this method of stewing you can use the following complements:

Bamboo shoots (rolling cut), to be added in the last 15 minutes. 24 oz.

White potato (rolling cut), to be added in the last 1/2 hour. 24 oz.

Brussels sprouts (whole), to be added in the last 15 minutes. 24 oz.

Turnips (rolling cut), to be added in the last 1/2 hour. 24 oz. Certain kinds of turnips take less time to cook. It may happen that the turnips will be cooked and the meat will still be tough. In this case, remove the turnips, continue stewing the meat until done, and return the turnips to the dish during the last one minute of cooking.

When the complements are added, increase the dark soy sauce accordingly and also add some salt.

The purpose of adding a complement in this dish is to absorb the excess fat from the meat. A little bit of spices can be used to make a variation - use the Five Fragrant Spices.

STEWED WHOLE PORK SHANK

For this dish, you should buy a shoulder roast cut. It is very important that the meat be completely covered with skin.

There are three ways to cook this dish:

With the first method, start by washing the roast. Put it in a cooking pot or casserole dish. For 3 pounds of shoulder roast use:

9 T. dark soy sauce
2 T. sugar
10 T. wine

Cover barely with water. Bring to a boil. Thicken with 1 tsp. cornstarch. You will not immediately notice the effect of the cornstarch, but it will produce a smooth gravy after the dish has been cooked more. The roast will be completely cooked after 1 to 1 1/2 hours - depending on the size of the cut. Be sure to turn the meat every 15 minutes. By the time the meat is tender, the gravy should measure about 1 cup. The gravy is ready when you have salted it to taste.

With the second method, brown the roast on all sides using 1/2 T. of oil, then add:

7 T. dark soy sauce
1 1/2 T. sugar
10 T. wine

Add no water, simmer at a very low heat until done (about 1 to 1 1/2 hours). Examine and turn roast every 15 minutes. Add several tablespoons of water - only if necessary. This method will produce much less gravy than the first.

With the third method, parboil the roast, wipe it dry, and rub all over with dark soy sauce. Deep fry at low heat until skin is golden brown. Rinse with cold water. Proceed as in the first method.

Comparisons: With the first method, the skin will be very soft and tender — almost melting in your mouth. With the second, the skin will be tender but chewy, and the gravy will have a stronger meaty flavor. With the third, the skin will be like a sponge — the fat will be less oily because of the parboiling and deep frying.

BEEF AND POTATO CAKES

This is a family dish (not for gourmet cooking) which is very much enjoyed by children. In this dish, ground meat is allowed.

8 oz. beef
8 oz. potatoes
1 small (3") onion chopped finely
1 egg yolk
1 T. soy sauce (dark)
1 tsp. salt

Cook the potatoes until just done. Peel (cook unpeeled) potatoes and mash. Mix in egg yolk and salt. Chop onion finely, brown with 1 T. oil, followed by ground meat. Brown for 4 minutes. Add soy sauce and mix this batch with the potatoes. Shape into balls the size of golf balls, flatten into cakes. Heat the cooking pan, grease lightly with oil, use medium heat to brown the cakes, turn to brown both sides.

If an electric skillet is available, set the temperature at 340°. When automatic control light blinks, turn to other side.

BEEF STRIPS CHINESE-FRIED WITH BEAN SPROUTS

8 oz. beef
4 oz. bean sprouts

Marinade for beef: regular

Bean sprouts should never be over-cooked, yet if not cooked enough, they will have a certain disagreeable smell. There are two ways to treat the bean sprouts for a standard Chinese-fry:

1 - Bring enough water to cover the bean sprouts to a boil. Immerse the bean sprouts in this boiling water for 10 seconds, drain immediately and start Chinese-fry.

2 - Using a dry wok, heat to a high temperature, drop in bean sprouts and toast (about 1/2 - 1 minute). Keep aside and procede with the Chinese-fry.

When the bean sprouts have been prepared in one of the above ways, add them to the beef strips when almost done, at the end of the Chinese-fry.

A small amount of soy sauce should be added according to the quantity of bean sprouts - or salt to taste.

BEEF STROGANOFF

I am not going to give you the complete recipe for Beef Stroganoff, I am only going to indicate simple modifications which will improve the texture of the meat.

Prepare sauce according to your preference and keep in a double boiler. Cut the beef in slices as normally used in Chinese-frying, then marinate with the following seasonings per pound:

1/4 tsp. salt
1 T. wine
1/8 tsp. pepper
1 T. cornstarch

5 minutes before serving, Chinese-fry the beef and when done, mix it with the sauce.

The beef will be very tender if cooked according to the Chinese method. Friends have thought that I used filet mignon when really it was only top round.

ROAST BEEF

There are many different techniques for preparing roast beef. Usually it is expected that the roast beef will be rare in the middle and well roasted on the outside. The amount of juices inside the roast are what will determine how well done it will be.

Marinate the beef with:

1 oz. wine mixed with 1 oz. water per pound
seasonings of your preference

Roast as usual. This will produce a tender, juicy beef. Use the leftover liquid for gravy.

The Chinese cook sometimes uses a very hot skillet to brown the beef all over which seals in the juices, and then puts it in the oven for roasting.

BEEF STRIPS CHINESE-FRIED WITH ONIONS

8 oz. beef
2 - 3" onions
1 T. soy sauce

Marinade for beef:

1 T. dark soy sauce
1 tsp. sugar
1 T. wine
1 T. cornstarch

Cut beef into strips and marinate. Procede with regular Chinese-fry.

Finishing touch: Add 1 tsp. wine, 1 tsp. cornstarch, and several drops sesame oil.

BEEF STRIPS CHINESE-FRIED WITH CELERY

8 oz. beef
8 oz. celery
1 tsp. sugar

Follow same procedure as for Beef Strips Chinese-Fried with Onions except add the sugar before the finishing touch.

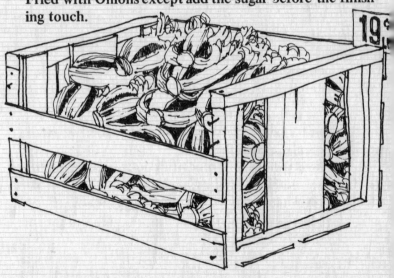

BEEF STRIPS CHINESE-FRIED WITH GREEN PEPPER

8 oz. beef
8 oz. green pepper

Marinade for beef: regular

In Chinese-frying, you use only the outer skin of the green pepper. Trim it as follows: cut the head off, cut into 4 pieces (from top to bottom; not around middle), remove membrane.

Cut the beef and green pepper into strips - marinate the beef. Then procede with the regular Chinese-fry procedure.

BEEF SLICES CHINESE-FRIED WITH BROCCOLI

8 oz. beef
8 oz. broccoli
1/4 tsp. salt
slice of ginger the size of a quarter

Marinade for beef: regular

Cut beef into slices and marinate. Trim broccoli to match beef in size - peel stem.

Using 1 T. oil, Chinese-fry the broccoli first, adding the salt, for 1-2 minutes. Sprinkle with water if the leaves start to burn. Set aside. Start Chinese-fry again with the beef. When 3/4 done, add broccoli and finish procedure.

Finishing touch: Mix together 1 tsp. cornstarch mixed with 1 T. water, and 1/2 T. light soy sauce. Use this mixture to thicken beef and broccoli. Add several drops of sesame oil and serve.

Add soy sauce and sugar to taste.

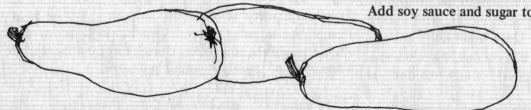

BEEF'S TONGUE

1/2 clove garlic
1 T. oil
2 T. cooking wine
2 T. dark soy sauce per pound of meat
1 tsp. sugar per pound of meat

Cooking tongue is often extended by the length of time it takes to remove the skin of the tongue. However, with patience and practice, removal of the skin won't take more than a few minutes. Here is a trick to remove the skin:

Bring a large quantity of water to a boil. Immerse the tongue completely and turn off the heat. After one minute, lift the tongue from the water and check to see if the skin is becoming loosened. As soon as the skin is loose, remove the tongue from the water and peel the skin off. Time is a critical factor as if the tongue is left in too long, it will be cooked through to the interior of the tongue. After skin has been removed, trim excess fat and dry with a paper towel. Use a blunt knife in peeling the skin from the tongue. If it cannot be peeled easily, the only other way is to cook it for another hour—as is usually done.

Brown garlic in oil, then brown tongue on both sides. Lower heat and add cooking wine. For each pound of tongue, add 2 T. dark soy sauce. Cook over low heat for 1 1/2 to 2 hours. Turn tongue at intervals of 20 minutes. Cook tongue with a very small quantity of moisture - no more than 6 to 8 tablespoonfuls of liquid. If liquid quantity is over this amount, increase heat to evaporate liquid. Conversely, if liquid is below 6 or 8 tablespoonfuls, add water. During last 20 minutes, add 1 teaspoon of sugar per pound and serve.

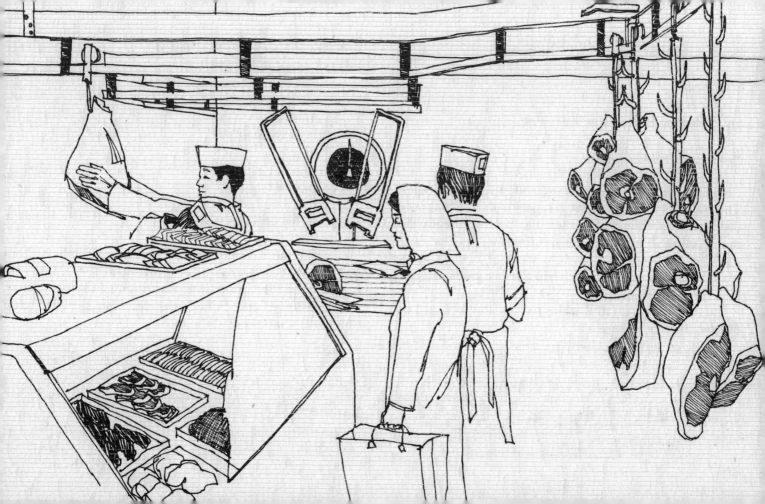

BEEF CHINESE-FRIED WITH LEEKS

8 oz. beef
4 oz. leeks
1/2 T. dark soy sauce per 4 oz. leeks

Marinade for beef: regular

The leek is very delicate and easily overcooked. The only special treatment in this standard Chinese-fry dish is to add the leeks when the beef is already 3/4 done, followed by seasoning and finishing touch.

The beef may be cut into slices or strips. Cut the leeks to match accordingly. Add the soy sauce after the leeks have been added.

Note: Use only the white part of the leek and cut diagonally. See picture.

BEEF SLICES CHINESE-FRIED WITH CAULIFLOWER

8 oz. beef
8 oz. cauliflower
1 1/2 T. dark soy sauce
1 tsp. sugar
1 tsp. cornstarch
1/4 cup water

Marinade for beef: regular

Trim the cauliflower and boil it for 5 minutes or more in salted water with 1 T oil added. Drain when it is cooked. At the same time, start your Chinese-fry with the cauliflower and follow with seasonings. Finish the Chinese-fry and serve.

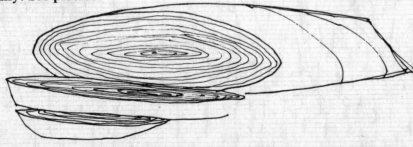

BEEF SLICES CHINESE-FRIED WITH CABBAGE

8 oz. beef
8 oz. cabbage
1 T. oil
1 tsp. salt
1 tsp. light soy sauce

Marinade for beef:

1 T. dark soy sauce
1 tsp. sugar
1 T. wine
1 T. cornstarch

Cabbage takes a longer time to cook than other vegetables. Start cooking it with the oil, salt and soy sauce till it is done. Cook the cabbage covered under medium heat. A little water may be necessary during the cooking. Set the cabbage aside, start Chinese-fry with the beef slices and add the cabbage at the end of the procedure when the meat is done. Thicken and serve.

83

BEEF SLICES CHINESE-FRIED WITH OYSTER SAUCE

This is a very popular basic dish for a beef Chinese-fry. When oyster sauce is used, only a limited selection of complements may be used. Some are: bamboo shoots, sugar peas, mustard greens, and asparagus.

8 oz. beef
8 oz. vegetable

Marinade for beef:

1 T. light soy sauce
1 tsp. sugar
1 T. wine
1 T. cornstarch

Procede with the standard Chinese-fry method. For the finishing touch use:

1 T. oyster sauce (per single portion)
1/2 T. dark soy sauce
1 tsp. sugar
1/2 T. cornstarch
5 T. water

Thicken and serve.

STEWED BEEF

24 oz. beef
4 1/2 T. soy sauce
1T. sugar
1 T. wine
2 slices ginger the size of a penny

Cut the beef into cubes 1" x 1" and simmer with water barely covering for 15 minutes. Drain beef and brown at medium temperature using 1 T. oil, and 1 clove of garlic. Add soy sauce, sugar, wine, and ginger. Add the drained juice; simmer at low heat until tender.

This is the general way of Chinese-stewing beef. Complements many be added during stewing.

Variation: These complements may be added if desired:

potatoes
turnips
brussels sprouts
carrots

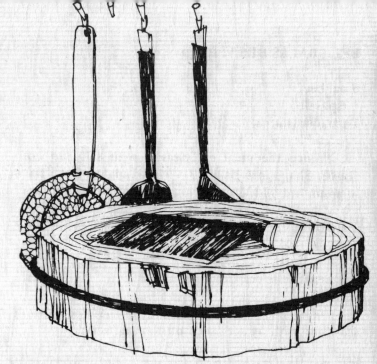

Another variation: Soy bean paste may be used instead of soy sauce. In this case, complements or vegetables are not desirable.

This dish is refered to by Western cooks as " Chinese goulash."

BEEF BALLS DEEP FRIED

8 oz. beef
1 tsp. salt
1 tsp. cornstarch

Mince the meat and season with salt and cornstarch. Shape into balls - 3/4" in diameter. Deep fry in medium hot oil (320°). Drain and serve.

Variation:

1/2 cup broth
oyster sauce to season

After beef balls have been deep fried, pour broth seasoned with oyster sauce on top and serve.

Another variation:

8 oz. spinach
1 T. oil
1 cup oyster sauce

Parboil the spinach in salted water with the oil added. Drain spinach, press lightly to remove moisture. Lay the spinach on a plate, arrange meat balls in the middle of the spinach leaving a margin of about 1" around the edge of the plate. Prepare 1 cup oyster sauce and pour on top.

Note: The oyster sauce for the meat balls should be thicker and not in a large quantity, while the oyster sauce for the spinach should be a little thinner and in a larger quantity. You must press the spinach to get rid of the excess water, thereby allowing the oyster sauce to be absorbed. Also, the excess water will not combine with the sauce and the sauce will simply float on top of the water.

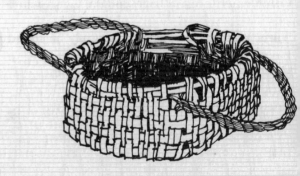

BEEF BALLS POACHED IN SPINACH SOUP

8 oz. beef
4 oz. spinach
4 cups meat broth (plain water can be used)

Marinade for beef:

1 1/2 T. light soy sauce
1 tsp. wine
1/8 tsp. pepper
1 tsp. cornstarch

Mince meat and marinate. Bring meat broth to a boil (plain water can also be used). Add seasonings as needed. Add spinach. Remove broth from heat. Shape meat into small balls about 3/4" in diameter. (see Pork Balls in Broth) Drop meat balls into broth and return to heat. Bring to a boil under low-medium heat.

Finishing touch: Sprinkle with several drops of sesame oil and serve.

Note: Poaching the meat balls away from the heat source allows for more even cooking and also prevents the boiling broth from breaking the balls.

87

FISH FAMILY STYLE (SHALLOW FRIED)

1 whole fish
2 tsp salt per pound of fish
1 T. oil
2 stalks green onion chopped finely
2 pieces ginger the size of a penny
1 T. light soy sauce
1 tsp. sugar
1 T. wine
2 T. water

Wipe the fish dry with a paper towel. Rub it well with salt (inside and out). Heat the wok at a high temperature, add oil, and tilt wok until all the bottom is coated with oil. Lower the heat to below medium setting. Do not disturb the fish. Tilt the wok at different angles to let the fish catch the heat evenly. Be patient and cook for about 10 minutes on each side. Drops of oil may occasionally be added if needed to prevent the fish from burning and sticking to the bottom of the wok. This cooking technique is called "shallow-frying". Turn the fish to the other side and repeat cooking procedure. When the fish is done (well browned), if the wok is apparently burned, take out the fish, clean the wok, and start again.

Add the green onion chopped finely with the ginger, soy sauce, sugar, wine, and water. Tilt the wok to let this mixture surround the fish - cook under medium heat for 1 minute. Turn the fish to the other side and cook for 1 minute - then serve.

STEAMED FISH

By Chinese standards, the fish that has more tiny bones will have a firmer texture in the meat and is the more suitable for steaming. It is no problem at all to eat fish that has many tiny bones with chopsticks, but to eat such a fish with a knife and fork is like the TV program - Mission Impossible!

1 whole fish
salt
one or two green onions
soy sauce
coriander
green onion chopped
ginger

Wipe the fish dry and rub with salt. Cut several pieces of the white part of an onion and use them as a rack to support the fish and keep it from touching the plate on which it is to be steamed. Lay the fish on top of the onions, the space left between the fish and the plate will allow the steam to completely surround the fish. Always start to steam a fish when the water in the steamer starts to boil. 10 minutes is about right for a small sized fish (about a foot in length). Garnish it with light soy sauce, coriander, chopped green onion, ginger, and 2 tsp. hot oil, then serve.

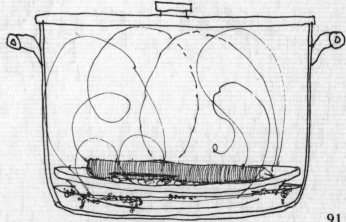

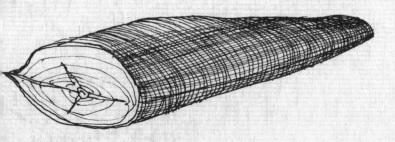

91

POACHED FISH

Chinese poach fish in hot water or broth - but only a whole fish will be used with this method of cooking. If the fish is cut in small sizes, much of the juice and taste of the fish will be lost if poached. When your recipe calls for small portions of fish, a steaming method is better than poaching. Save the juice from the steaming to make a sauce.

1 whole fish
1 tsp. salt
2 stalks green onion
2 pieces ginger root the size of a quarter
1/2 oz. coriander
2-3 T. oil
1 T. light soy sauce

Bring enough water to cover fish to a boil. (The fish must be covered completely, leaving at least 1" of water over the fish.) Lower the boiling water to just under the boiling point. Immerse the fish well under the

93

water. Cover and keep at the lowest possible heat for 10 minutes (for a fish that is about a foot long). Then take the fish out with two spatulas. Lay the fish on a plate and sprinkle with the salt.

Have ready the onion, ginger root, and coriander. Cut all these into fine strips and use them to garnish the top of the fish. Heat the oil until it smokes, then pour it on top of the garnish. Add the soy sauce and serve.

FISH QUICK STEWED

1 large fish
1 T. wine
3 T. dark soy sauce per pound of fish
2 tsp. cornstarch
1 1/2 tsp. sesame oil

A large fish is desirable for this dish. Shallow-fry the fish lightly on both sides. Add in the wine, soy sauce, sugar, and enough water to barely cover the fish. Bring to a boil at a high temperature. Tilt the wok from time to time to prevent the fish from sticking. Turn to other side and cook. Keep on reducing the liquid until it is about 1/2 cup. Take the fish out and put it on a plate. Thicken the remaining sauce with cornstarch and sesame oil. Pour on top of the fish and serve.

Variation: During the reducing time, bean curd would be a very good addition to the quick stew.

FISH SOUP

1 fish (fresh water)
1 T. wine
water to cover
2 small pieces of ginger
small amount of white part of green onion

Fresh water fish should be used for this soup, and you may use the leftover bone from a fish fillet you have already used.

Use lard to brown the bone or whole fish lightly on both sides. Turn heat up to high and add wine, followed immediately by water to cover the fish. Add in ginger an and onion. Simmer at low heat for about 30 minutes then add some white pepper, salt to taste, and serve.

FISH FILLET SOUP

fillet of fresh fish
1/4 tsp. wine
1/8 tsp. pepper
1 tsp. oil
a little chopped ginger, green onion, or coriander
4 cups broth
sesame oil

A fresh fish fillet is desirable for this soup. Cut it into thin slices (if the fillet is thick it should be trimmed to make it thinner). Arrange the fish slices in a soup bowl and mix with wine, pepper, salt, oil and ginger. Do not pack all the ingredients together. Pour boiling broth on top, several drops of sesame oil, and serve.

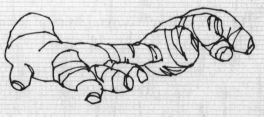

95

PRAWNS QUICK-STEWED

1/2 lb. prawns
1 T. wine
1 1/2 T. dark soy sauce
2 tsp. sugar
1 piece ginger root the size of a penny
water
1 stalk green onion quartered
1 tsp. cornstarch
1 T. oil

Shallow-fry the prawns until both sides are browned. Add the wine, soy sauce, sugar, ginger root and barley cover with water. Add quartered onion. Cook covered for 10 minutes under medium heat. Stir and continue cooking until the liquid has reduced to 1/2 its original quantity. Thicken it with cornstarch and serve.

Finishing touch: Several drops of sesame oil.

PRAWNS DRY-FRIED

1/2 lb. prawns
1 stalk chopped onion
2 pieces ginger root the size of a quarter
1/2 clove garlic
2 tsp. oil per pound
wine
1 tsp. sugar

Leaving the shell intact, cut a very tiny slit on the back side of the prawns and remove the membrane. Wipe dry and deep fry for 2 to 3 minutes, until brown. Drain the prawns. Start again in the same wok with the onion, ginger root and garlic. Add in the prawns. Toss constantly to let the seasonings penetrate the shell evenly. Add oil and sprinkle with wine 2 or 3 times with intervals of 10 seconds. Keep on tossing. The purpose of the wine is to soak the dissolved salt into the prawns. It also prevents the prawn from burning, as by now the wok is almost dry. Therefore, the exact amount of wine is not essential as long as no apparent liquid is left in the wok. Add the sugar just before serving.

Finishing touch: Sprinkle with sesame oil.

TIME FISH

I tried to find the name of this fish in English, but in vain.

The Time Fish swim yearly down the Yang-tze River and when they approach the sea, they turn and swim back upstream. When they approach the Nanking area, they are just matured. When the first Time Fish is caught, the old tradition is to dedicate it to the mayor of the city, who was referred to as the Parent of the City -- may all mayors deserve this dedication.

All fish, if strong enough, will carry on their journey up to the Hopei area, where the Yang-tze River can be both wild and calm - where they spawn.

I mention Time Fish because of the special way in which they are prepared. It is the only fish that is cooked without the scales being removed. The Time Fish has shining silver scales. They are very oily and the fat is delicious -- without any fishy smell. The meat is also very tender and fatty. It was reported that when these fish were caught in the net, they did not fight and move just as though they did not want to hurt their precious scales.

The standard seasoning for this fish is rice-vinegar

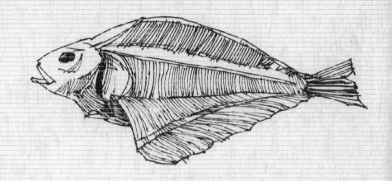

with soy sauce. This seasoning can also be used for salmon as the salmon is also a fatty fish and it blends well in taste.

The best way to prepare a fresh fish is by steaming. The fish will maintain its deliciousness and no cook can cheat with an unfresh fish in steaming. Because of this, a true gourmet will always refuse a sweet and sour fish in restaurants as the cooks might cheat you, using the sweet and sour taste to cover up the fact that the fish is not fresh. You don't have to cheat anyone in your kitchen, but if you ever have to use a fish that is not quite fresh, you can always prepare it using sweet and sour sauce.

FRESH FISH

Chinese care very much about the freshness of food, especially when buying fish. In Hongkong you can not only buy many kinds of live fish, but also many kinds of rare fish -- a "monkey cod" a foot in length is sold at a price of sixty five dollars. There are also live prawns and shrimp, which are almost impossible to find in many other parts of the world.

The freshness of fish and seafood is essential, as their meat is firmer, there is less fishy smell, and the taste is naturally sweet. That is why in Chinatown in San Francisco, there are so many fish shops that have tanks full of live fish, as demanded by Chinese gourmets.

To distinguish a fresh fish is very simple. The eyes should be full and transparent, the body firm and strong looking, not s-o-f-t feeling. The gills should never be darker in color. A male carp will have a slim body, while the female carp will have a full belly, this will leave a slight difference in weight after trimming.

TO COOK FISH WITH PLENTIFUL TINY BONES

This is a famous dish in Soo-chow, which by common opinion, is the best place to be born in China. Most people think that this is so because Soo-chow is famous for beautiful girls. But it is not for this reason that Soo-chow is the best place to be born -- it is because the peo-

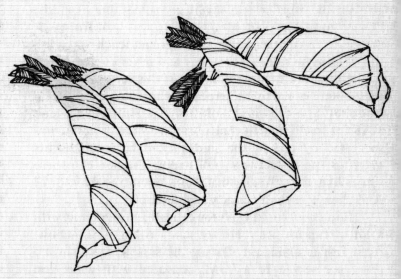

ple of Soo-chow are deeply affectionate and care very much for their children. Soo-chow dialect is a very soft tone and when spoken by a woman, it can attract men almost to the stage of a hypnotic trance. Spoken by men, it is somewhat "sissy." Most Soo-chownese men try to avoid their native dialect. It is rather delightful to quarrel with a Soo-chownese as when they quarrel with a stronger opponent, in order to save face and yet not give in, the weaker one might say something like this: "Okay you little devil, don't run away -- wait for me, I am going to call my uncle to come and teach you a lesson!" Then he calmly goes away and never comes back.

One more famous story about this very soft dialect tells about a northern sergeant who came to direct a troop of Soo-chownese soldiers. His strong command MARCH made no effect. He was astonished, and it was suggested by one of the soldiers that he take over his place, as the dialect was so different. The Soo-chownese spoke like this: "Will you fellows mind marching on?" And then everybody neatly marched off.

Soo-chow cooking is very delicate, elegant, and with a lot of caprice. As there are many rivers in Soo-chow, fresh fish is abundant. During the season, fresh shrimp (live) are served in a bowl, activated with wine, and covered with another bowl. The shrimps start to jump inside the bowls. Then, after a minute or so, they are quiet -- intoxicated.

This is the famous "Drunken Shrimp," and is served with soy sauce and fermented bean curd paste. The meat tastes sweet and has no fishy smell.

For fish with plentiful tiny bones, carp can be used. It should be small -- about six inches long. I have tried this with many different kinds of fish. As long as it has firm meat, the tiny bones will be no problem.

Clean the fish, wipe dry and brown both sides with a little oil. Using a small sized pot, lay a bunch of green onions at the bottom, cut in half lengthwise. Arrange the fish on top and allow 1 1/2 T. dark soy sauce, 1 1/2 T. sugar, and 3 T. malted vinegar per each 8 oz. of fish. Add water to barely cover and simmer under a low heat until the liquid is reduced to half the original amount. Bring out the fish and onion and rearrange them in the bottom of the pan with the onions on top this time. Return the remaining liquid to the pan and simmer again until no more than several tablespoons of sauce are left. Generally, the long simmering and the vinegar will make the bones edible. This is sometimes served as a side dish, cold, with plain rice "congee" for breakfast.

RICE

There are many many methods of cooking rice. There are even several methods of cooking rice without using cookware. Waterlily leaves coated with mud and roasted on an open fire can be used, also fresh big bamboo trunks.

As every different kind of rice has a different capacity for absorbing moisture, how much water you should use depends on your personal preference. However, in general, for a small portion which serves 4 to 6, the water should be about one inch above the rice in the pot when you start. The size of the cooking pot also plays an important part. You should never cook rice filled too full in the pot as it needs some space for the steam to do the cooking job. Also, too big a pot for too little rice will leave too much empty space, which cools the steam.

The most common style of cooked rice is seasonless, oilless rice. The cooking process for this type of rice is as follows:

Bring the water and rice to a boil with a cover. Remove the cover and leave on high heat. (You might not agree with this.) Now give it a thorough stir. (You might not agree with this also.) If the water was used in too large an amount, it doesn't really matter very much. If it was used in too little an amount, you should increase it at this time. This can be determined by looking at the rice - it should be almost 3/4 swelled. It will not be cooked unless you simmer it for another 10 minutes. The right time to start simmering is when no apparent water is still on top of the rice, and a lot of chimneys or vents have formed. (You might have to wait a little while.) Never stir the rice at this moment, which will close the vents and the steam will not work completely.

To wash or not to wash the rice? I can only tell you that completely washed rice tends to be less sticky. The easiest way to wash the rice is to use a wire whisk. Just stir the rice with the whisk under tap water, in a few minutes you will have the rice washed without weting your hands.

The type of wire whisk to be used should be the one that resembles a section of a metal spring.

RICE

Rice is the greatest single food product of China, and, as such, is held in great esteem. Its cultivation is a tedious, time consuming job, and would tax the patience of any people.

Necessity has taught the Chinese this patience, however, each farmer has a companion to ease his load, keep him company, and be his partner in this tedious but essential task.

The water buffalo is all these things and more. He is transportation, tractor, and a sign of wealth. What could be more fitting, my friends, than treating him like the friend he is? This deserved veneration of the water buffalo is one of the reasons for the lack of beef dishes in most of China. Only on occasion, for religious purposes, does beef appear. For instance, some older people still refuse beef and may eat or purchase foods at Moslem restaurants.

SMOKED EGGS

Only middle-aged Chinese who have lived in Eastern China will not be surprised by this dish. The original dish calls for geese eggs, I figured out that the only reason is because they are bigger in size which makes them easier to half-boil.

Smoked eggs are used as a cold dish, served mostly in wine-houses as appetizers with drinks.

Use choice large sized eggs and try boiling them in your own way - but the yolk is expected to be soft and uncooked. I do it in my own clumsy way, because I want to be sure that the yolk is soft and the white is cooked. Boil the eggs for 3 1/2 minutes, then cool them in tap water until completely cold. Cook again for 3 1/2 minutes and cool again. This leaves no chance for the yolk to be cooked.

I hope you have the looo, or otherwise you will have to use soy sauce mixed with water and sugar to make a comparable substitute. Heat the looo to a boil, cool it down to 180°, immerse the eggs (without shells) overnight. By the next morning, the eggs will be dark in color, and will have absorbed quite an amount of seasoning and flavoring from the looo.

104

Bring the eggs out, arrange them on a rack, and follow by smoking for 5 minutes. Cut the eggs into wedges, sprinkle with looo and sesame oil and serve.

Hint: Before serving, examine one egg. The yolk should be soft but not runny. If it is runny, heat the looo to a boil and immerse egg for 1 or 2 minutes more.

PUFF EGGS SOUP

2 eggs
1/2 tsp. salt
1 stalk chopped green onion
4 cups broth or water

Beat eggs with salt and onion. Heat wok to a high temperature. Add in 1 tsp. oil and pour in beaten eggs. When the bottom side is firm, turn to other side. After another 10 seconds, add in broth or water. Bring to a boil and serve.

BEAN CURD AND EGGS

3 eggs, beaten
1 tsp. salt
1 tsp. oil
1/8 tsp. pepper
1/2 cup bean curd

Dice the bean curd into 1/4" x 1/4" size. Soak in a cup of water with 2 tsp. salt added for 10 minutes. Drain and brown using 3 T. oil, move the pan to help in browning. When browned on all sides, add in beaten eggs with salt, oil and pepper. Stir gently until eggs become firm. Chopped green onion may be added in at the last 1/2 minute before serving.

EGGS AND TOMATO

3 eggs
1 tsp. salt
1 tsp. oil
1/8 tsp. pepper
1 tomato (3" - 4" in size)

Beat eggs with salt, oil, and pepper. Cut tomato into 8 wedges. Sprinkle with a little salt and coat with cornstarch on sides without skin. Heat a flat pan, using a little oil, brown the tomato on the sides without skin. It only takes a few seconds for the starch to settle firm, then add in the beaten eggs. Turn heat up to high, stir gently, folding eggs with the tomato until the eggs are just firm, and serve.

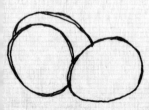

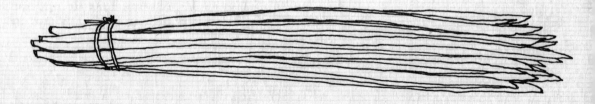

FROZEN BEAN CURD AND FROZEN EGGS

Freeze the normal bean curd until it almost reaches the frozen state. Do not let it freeze completely or it will become too flaky. Thaw it again and cut into cubes, and then slices. This is very interesting for stewing. The texture of the bean curd will be like a sponge - it absorbs more seasoning than the normal bean curd.

Using the same principal, I once tried this with a boiled egg. It also comes out spongy. I loooed it and called it the "Eskimo's Eggs".

Hard boil the eggs, keep them in the freezer with the shell, thaw them and looo them or stew with soy sauce.

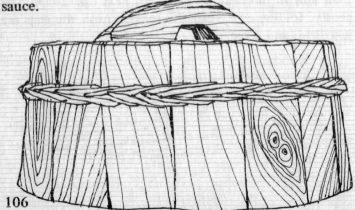

EGG-CAKE BAKED IN A WOK

1 cup eggs
1 tsp. salt
1 tsp. oil
2 stalks green onion, chopped

This is a very practical dish for a variety in egg dishes.

Beat eggs with salt, oil and onion. Heat the wok, not too hot, and add 1 T. oil. Tilt the wok around and around until the oil coats the entire cooking area of the wok. Pour in the beaten eggs. Lower the heat to medium low and cover the batch with a small lid - just big enough to cover the eggs. Wait for several minutes then add in a few drops of oil around the edge of the lid. Repeat after a few minutes. The eggs should be firm after about 6 to 10 minutes. Take the eggs out and serve upside down on a plate, cut diagonally into strips 3/4" x 1 1/2" in size.

SHRIMP CHIPS

You can make your own home made shrimp chips with which no one can compare. Here is the recipe for non-commercial shrimp chips:

1 lb. net weight of shelled shrimp, prawns or lobster
1 lb. tapioca flour
1 oz. salt
1 tsp. white pepper powder
1 cup water

Bring water to a boil and dissolve salt and pepper powder. Pour boiling water onto the tapioca flour in a large mixing bowl and stir quickly with a cooking spoon. Add in the shrimp and knead as a dough. As the water content of the shrimp is unpredictable, you may adjust it by adding more boiling water. The dough should be on the hard side. Now shape into a tube about 1" in diameter. If you do not have the proper steamer for this process, a bamboo rack or cake cooling rack will do. Lay a cheesecloth underneath and on top of the dough and place it on the rack. Make sure the tubes of dough are far enough apart (at least 1 1/2" if space permits) to prevent them from sticking together. Steam at a high temperature for 45 minutes. Make sure there is plenty of water in the steamer to avoid having to open it to add more water.

After the steaming, bring out, remove the cheesecloth, and cool the dough on another rack. Keep in a cool place to dry. The time varies from 1 day to 2 or 3 days. If you can cut it with a very sharp knife, then start to cut it into thin slices (about the thickness of a penny). Now lay the slices on a piece of cardboard and dry in the sun until brittle. Don't hurry the drying before you cut them.

You can store them indefinitely in a can. When you want to use them, calculate 2 or 3 chips per person. Deep fry in oil at 360° temperature. If the process has been done correctly, the chips will be done in a matter of seconds. They will increase their size several times. Drain and serve.

Use them as a garnish for crispy fried chicken or duck etc. You can also use them as hors d'oeuvres or as appetizers.

BEAN CURD AND SPINACH

Spinach is nick-named "The Parrot" in Chinese, owing to its pinkish point at the end, and the leaves are green like the feathers of a parrot.

There is a Chinese legend about this dish — it goes like this: Once a king was visiting a mountain village. He dressed as a commoner to investigate how life really was among his people.

He stopped at a shabby wine-house. (Wine-houses serve simple food or appetizers with wine.) They, especially in the mountains, have a flag pole out in front of the house. The flag indicates whether or not wine is available, to avoid customers' coming from a distance only to be told that the wine is sold out. (How thoughtful of these small traders!) A beautiful young girl attended the king.

Caught by her extreme beauty and innocent charm, the king tried to find words to start a conversation with this shy but intelligent girl.

"Young sister, please prepare for me a catty (about 20 oz.) of your best wine, and I would like it very warm." (Rice wines are served warm.)

"Yes, sir, we just have opened a jar of wine that my father brewed ten years ago." While the girl was busy warming the wine, the king's eyes followed her like a pair of searchlights - what bad manners for a king! But he was a man. After a few minutes, the girl brought the wine to the table, walking as a summer evening breeze.

"Young sister, the wine is cool," without sipping, the king tried to find something to complain about.

"Sir, maybe you are referring to the wine cup, I think the wine is just warm."

"Oh, yes, good wine, very good wine!" The king gulped the whole cup. "Now, can you bring me something to eat?"

"Well, in this poor mountain, we have only some vegetables and bean curd to offer, what about a Bean Curd Quick-Stewed, sir?"

"Umm, I like bean curd, but I would like it to be prepared with some meat, because I never eat a dish without meat."

"I am sorry sir, we haven't got any meat." Seeing the situation, the king seemed to enjoy seeing how the girl would react to his insisting on a dish with meat.

"Well, that is your problem!" He almost revealed his being a king by his attitude. "I WANT you to bring me a dish with any kind of meat, or I WILL be very angry!" Astonished and bothered by the king's stupidness, the girl thought for a while and said:

"I am sorry, I beg your pardon, ah! oh! yes, my father had a pheasant this morning, but it was sold to Uncle Wong, how about letting me prepare you a Bean Curd with Parrot, sir?"

"Do you eat parrots?"

"Oh, yes, it is a very delicious dish, sir."

Partly out of curiosity, and partly because he remembered his words of "any kind" of meat, he agreed and promised her a reward if the dish pleased him.

Bean Curd and Spinach was served, and the king was delighted!

Now let's get back to the recipe!

16 pieces bean curd — not the softer kind, each about 1" x 2" x 1/4"
8 oz. spinach cut into 2" lengths
1/2 clove garlic
1 T. soy sauce (light or dark)
1/2 tsp. salt
1 tsp. sugar

Dissolve 1 tsp. salt in cold water (enough to barely cover bean curd) for 10 minutes. The salt will solidify the protein of the bean curd and make it easier to brown for you.

Now drain the bean curd. Use 1 T. oil in a flat pan (a teflon pan is good in this case), and brown the bean curd on both sides to a light golden brown color. If you can not manage to work with a pair of chopsticks in turning the bean curd, it is a pity when Chinese cooking. You can use the tip of a knife or fork in this case.

Add in soy sauce, sugar, and 1/4 cup of water. (In this dish broth is not desirable as a plain vegetable taste is more pleasing than a meaty taste.) Simmer for 5 to 10 minutes, then set aside.

Start again with a clean wok and Chinese-fry the spinach using 3 T. oil, adding in the garlic and salt. When the spinach is almost done, add in the cooked bean curd. Quick-stew it for a minute or two. Thicken the sauce with 1 tsp. cornstarch before serving and add several drops of sesame oil, of course!

This is a wonderful family dish. A fancy dish is good only once in a while, while a simple dish such as this may be used many times during the week without dulling your appetite. I mentioned that plain water is even better than meat broth. It is like an innocent girl without even lipstick. If you understand this, you not only know much in cooking, but also know much about make-up.

BEAN CURD

The soy bean is known as the "Wonderful Bean" in China. Without its being so wonderful, I really don't know how poor people could obtain their necessary daily protein.

Bean curd is only one of the several hundred by-products of the soy bean. In simple words, bean curd is like fresh cottage cheese which is made from the milk of the cow — bean curd is made from the milk of the soy bean.

Here is how bean curd is made: The soy beans are first soaked overnight, then ground up with water to form a "milk." This "milk" is then filtered through cloth. Then the "milk" is brought to a boil; settling agents, such as alkali salt, can be added slowly. Then the curd will form. The curd is separated from the residue and wrapped in a cloth and pressed with a weight.

The moisture content will determine the type of bean curd — soft, medium, or hard.

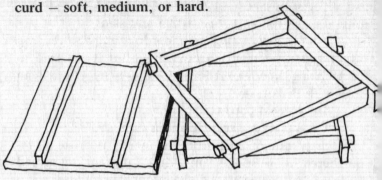

In the traditional home of China, a stone "quern" or grinder is used to grind up the beans with lots of water being used. This liquid mixture of ground beans and water drops into a wooden barrel with projections on the inside. These projections hold a perforated wooden disk that is covered with a crude type of cheesecloth. The cheesecloth strains the ground liquid mass of large particles. The residue of these particles or "mash" is then gathered up in the cloth and the excess water is squeezed into the tub. The "mash" is returned to the grinder for a second time. What is left after the second squeezing is used as feed for livestock.

A chemical such as powdered gypsum or even sour soy vinegar is added and the combination brought to a boil. The heat and chemical cause coagulation of the litquid. It is now returned to the barrel and the excess water drained off. A round closely-meshed basket is pressed down into the liquid and more water rises up through the holes to be ladled off. After repeated ladling, the curds are spooned, with cloth in the bottom, into a type of press or "frame." The two frames, one on top of the other, are placed on a board and the fluid previously removed from the barrel is ladled into the frames. The edges of the cloth are folded over the open top and a weight is placed on a board the size of the frame. This board and weight cause an even pressure on the mass, straining out excess moisture through the sides of the cheesecloth. After half an hour or so, the weight and frames may be disassembled, leaving a mass similar in appearance to egg custard. If allowed to stand in the air, this mass will lose its moisture until sufficiently solid to be sliced into cakes and sold or stored. Storing fresh bean curd, or "tou-fu" under water in the refrigerator preserves its freshness -- water should be changed daily.

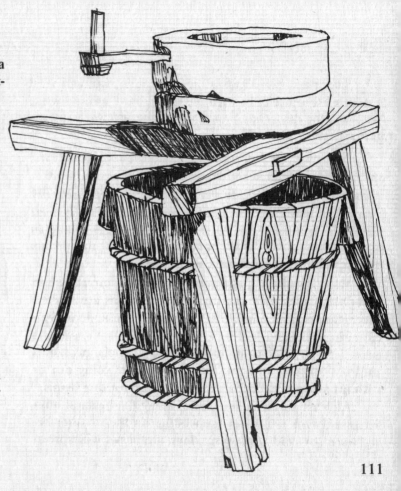

BEAN SPROUTS

There are two kinds of bean sprouts, although Westerners are familiar only with the mung bean sprouts which are used for dishes such as Chop Suey or sometimes as a garnish.

Soy bean sprouts have many more uses in the kitchen. They make a delicious soup which can stand a long simmering without losing its form. They can be stewed, Chinese-fried, or chopped and cooked with meat which is a popular Cantonese family dish. A Shanghai standard vegetable dish consists of soy bean sprouts stewed with deep fried bean curd diced.

Many families make their own bean sprouts when not obtainable from the market. The beans are soaked overnight, wrapped in cloth or kept in a colander covered with cloth, and left in a dark place. This phenomena is used to describe someone who had financial problems and was staying at home silently without going out or without any activity. Chinese say he is sprouting beans.

At least three or four times a day the beans should be rinsed with tap water, depending on the weather being warm or cold. In several days the beans will sprout to edible size. If the beans are covered with some weight, the bean sprouts will be stronger and bigger in size as they will have to struggle sprouting out. Without any weight they are free to grow lazily and become weak and small. A good lesson for parents for their children!

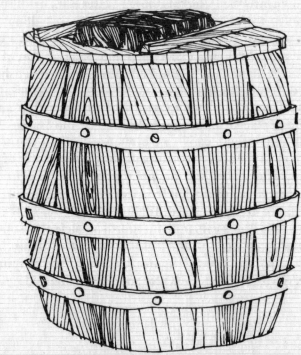

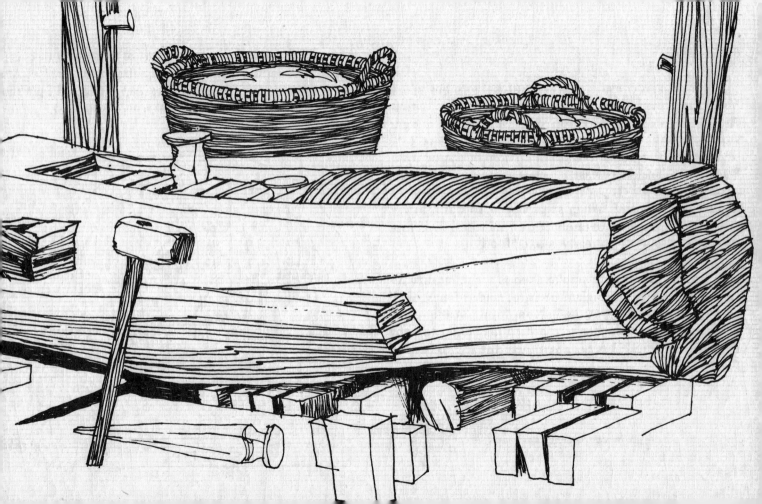

SMOKING

Smoking is considered a professional job, but many housewives can do their own smoking. A wok is first choice for smoking but you can use a large tin can. Don't use aluminum cookware as it will burn. Place 1 T. sugar and 1 T. black or red tea in bottom of can or wok. Place a rack inside at least 2 inches above tea and sugar. Arrange food on top of rack, cover, place on fire at highest temperature. When sugar begins to burn, lower heat, leave for approximately 2 to 5 minutes. This method is used only for already cooked food.

The large Chinese smoke oven is a community affair. It is shaped like a giant beehive, made of clay, with an igloo type opening at the bottom front. At the rear is an access door through which a man may enter to hang the various meats. There is a vent near the top to control the draft.

The main feature is that a lot of meat may be cured with just a little fuel. Also, since the meats are isolated from the fire, the fats and juices drip into a sand pit and prevent acrid smoke from re-entering the meats.

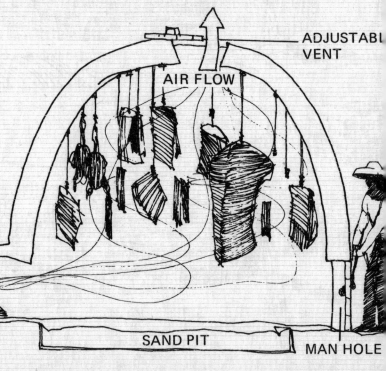

ADJUSTABLE VENT

AIR FLOW

AIR

FIRE

SAND PIT

MAN HOLE

114

QUICK-STEWING

When a certain dish calls for meats to be cut into chunks, a quick-stew is a good technique to use, perhaps preceeded by a Chinese-fry.

In a Chinese-fry you cannot have the meat in thick chunks and still cook them in 2 to 3 minutes. Therefore, in this case you would add a certain amount of water or stock, cover the pan and cook the meat over a high heat. This is called quick-stewing. It generally takes 15 minutes.

A quick-stewing can be done using plenty of soy sauce. Eventually the color will be reddish dark brown. Many restaurants call this RED Stewed. (It sounds as if it were prepared by a communist!)

Before serving, a quick-stew should always be thickened to a denser consistency. When soy sauce is not used, it is sometimes called White-Stewed. In this book, I simply use the word Stew.

NOODLES CHINESE-FRIED

Cook the noodles, rinse with cold water, drain. Add 1 T. oil per pound of noodles. Keep in refrigerator until use. Addition of oil will prevent noodles from sticking together. Reheat the noodles in a skillet or in oven at medium heat (about 300°). Turn noodles so they will brown evenly. Choose any Chinese-fry dish in which meat is cooked in strips or slices. For instance, pork strips with bamboo shoots or beef with green pepper. For variation vegetables can be added. Noodles can be arranged on the plate and the Chinese-fried meat dish, with lots of sauce, poured on top, or noodles can be added in at the end of the Chinese-frying. The second cooking method should not have as much sauce.

115

BASE

To "base" in Chinese cooking means to have a layer of vegetables underneath a batch of meat. I wonder if the one who invented "base" was a dietician because the plateful of meat looks like a large amount, yet most of it is the vegetables underneath.

This is nothing strange to Americans. Here you can order a turkey dinner for 99 cents, very inexpensive, not even a dollar! They will bring you a plate with what looks like a lot of turkey, but really there will only be two thin slices of meat with a dumpling underneath.

CIRCLE

To "circle" in Chinese cooking means to arrange the complement around the principal meat. In many cases, a whole chicken or shank of pork looks very lonely by itself on a plate. Therefore, choose a complement to circle around it. It increases the amount of food and improves its appearance — choose a complement of a contrasting color.

MINCING

To buy ground meat from a butcher is unacceptable to a gourmet Chinese cook. The reason for this is that the system of the grinding machine spoils the texture of the meat by squeezing it.

The housewife can only mince her meat by chopping as a proper machine is much too expensive for household use (about $599.95).

Procedure:

First trim the meat: remove nerves, gristle.
Cut into thin slices, then strips, then small bits.
Chop the bits finely with two knives. After 20-30 chops, turn the chopping board 1/4 of a turn and chop again - repeat until board is back to its original position. Turn over the whole batch of meat and chop again. The quality of the chop (i.e. fine, coarse, etc.) varies according to the recipe.

Hint: Wet your knives occasionally to prevent sticking. Try to adopt a rhythm with your hands to make the job more interesting and less tedious.

KNOW YOUR HEATING LIMIT

Many times an amateur singer at an informal party will get into trouble because he did not check his range of pitch against the music called for. When a note is out of range, it sounds bad. If you are not obliged to sing a certain song, choose one which is within your range.

Your family cooking heat is too weak by restaurant standards. But you can find out your limit and use the right amount of food for each Chinese fry accordingly. When cooking a large amount of food, I suggest you do the Chinese-fry in two batches. It will take you only another five minutes including the cleaning of the wok. If you insist on doing it in one batch, you will probably sing an off-key note.

When a larger party is to be handled, it will be rather too troublesome to have one Chinese-fried dish divided into three, four, of five batches. But this is very simple — why don't you just avoid Chinese-frying? For large parties try steaming, stewing, cold-mixing, deep-frying, etc. instead.

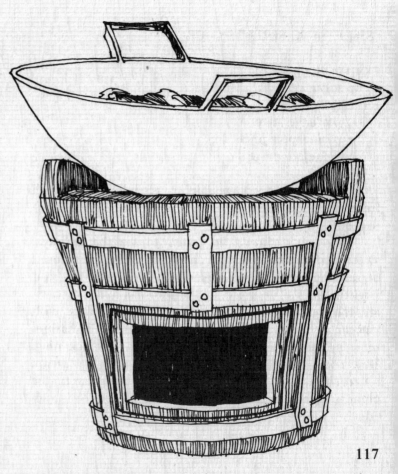

117

"SWEET AND SOUR" SAUCE

1 cup malt vinegar
1 cup sugar
1 1/2 T. salt
1/2 cup orange juice
1/2 cup pineapple juice
1/2 cup tomato paste

Fresh frozen orange juice is acceptable, although fresh is best. Combine the above ingredients and bring to a boil slowly. Simmer for 10 minutes.

The sauce should be tested to see the saltiness, sweetness, and sourness are all blended. Use the amount of salt indicated. It will never be over salted - but you might need a little more. If the sourness and sweetness are too heavy on one side, adjust the seasonings with vinegar or sugar. The resulting sauce should be harmoniously blended. Now prepare cornstarch for thickening. Determine the right consistency that a normal cream sauce should be. Before you add the cornstarch, the color is usually unappealing. When the cornstarch is added, the color will be somewhat like ketchup.

Storing: Keep this sauce in a large mouthed jar covered loosely to prevent anything from getting inside. Do not cover tightly because acid gasses will accumulate inside the jar and then pop out when it is opened. Do not store in the refrigerator because condensation will occur and eventually mould will form. Keep it in a cool dark place. It keeps well for months.

SWEET AND SOUR PORK

8 oz. boneless pork
1/2 tsp. salt
1 tsp. light soy sauce
flour
egg yolk
1 firm 3" tomato
1 - 3" onion
green pepper
1 doz. or so pineapple chunks
1/2 cup "sweet and sour" sauce

Cut boneless pork into 3/4" cubes. Season with salt and light soy sauce. Roll in all purpose flour. Roll again in egg yolk. Roll again in flour. Deep fry until done at 320° (2-3 minutes). Cut tomato into 8 parts. Cut onion the same way. Chop some green pepper into 3/4" x 3/4" squares - to be used for coloring purpose only.

When the pork is done, drain it. Using the same cooking wok or pan (you don't need to clean it), brown onion and pepper in 1 T. oil for 1/2 minute. Add in 1/2 cup "sweet and sour" sauce, cook for 1 minute. Add in tomato and pineapple chunks, cook for 5 seconds. Add the deep fried pork and take away from the heat. Mix well and serve immediately.

SWEET AND SOUR PORK RIBS (SHANGHAI STYLE)

When restaurants trim their own meat, they always leave plenty of meat on the ribs as this is more desirable to customers. However, as you may find that the ribs you buy in a store will be mostly bone, you can use pork chops cut into pieces instead.

12 oz. pork ribs
1 tsp. salt

Prepare the ribs exactly as for the Sweet and Sour Pork, except you should omit the egg yolk. The rest is done in a typical Shanghai style presentation. Only the "sweet and sour" sauce will be used in the last step. No tomato, pineapple, onion or peppers will be used. The sauce should be thicker and cover the pork ribs well. 1 tsp. dark soy sauce may be mixed with the "sweet and sour" sauce.

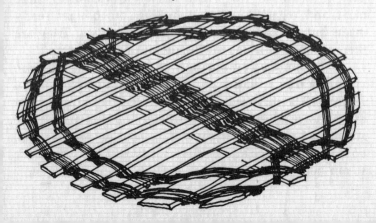

SWEET AND SOUR FISH

The fish to be used for this recipe should be one with very few tiny bones, such as cod.

1 whole fish
2 tsp. salt per pound of fish
all purpose flour
1/2 onion, chopped
1 cup "sweet and sour" sauce

Do not remove head and tail of fish -- wipe dry with a paper towel. Cut 5 slits diagonally on both sides of the fish to make it deep fry evenly. Rub all over with salt and dust with flour. Deep fry until dark brown and crispy.

Lay the fish on a plate. Use the same frying pan with 1 T. oil to brown the onion. (Chopped green or red peppers or cooked carrots cut into pea size can be added to enhance the appearance.) Add the "sweet and sour" sauce and bring to a boil at a high temperature for 1 minute. Pour sauce over fish to cover completely and serve.

DEEM SUM

Another use for the wok pan is as a support for steaming trays or racks. The wok is placed over the heat source and partially filled with water. Circular bamboo trays that fit snugly together are placed in the wok over the water. As many as eight racks or trays may be used in this manner, although three racks plus the lid are usually the limit for home use. These racks are usually filled with a variety of dumpling-like cakes called "Deem Sum." A tight fitting lid is placed on the top rack and the water in the wok is brought to a boil. In most cases, 15 to 20 minutes of steaming is all that is needed to prepare a lunch for the whole family. Quite often these meat and vegetable filled dumplings are bought ready made but uncooked in small specialty shops. They are then steamed at home during the normal meal time.

The unique combination of wok pan and bamboo steaming tray is native to China and has many unusual features. The main value is the ability to cook many separate things at once with the same amount of fuel. Since steam rises vertically, it passes through the various racks, cooking each piece on all sides as it rises. Thus, very little steam heat or energy is lost and the fuel requirement is kept low, as only the bottom of the pan where the boiling water is needs to be heated.

The racks themselves are hand made from layer upon layer of bamboo laminated together. This heavy layer construction insulates the rack and even keeps the food warm until serving time. As a matter of fact, some of the more elegant restaurants bring the racks directly to the table from the wok pan in the kitchen and serve only a small quantity of the contents. The lid is then replaced, and the racks keep the unserved portion warm on the table until needed.

It is more usual, however, for a restaurant to have a specially built stove with gas fired wok pans up to 40 inches in diameter. These pans accept stacks of steaming trays eight or ten high, and up to 36 inches around. Large hoods are then lowered down on to the woks and hundreds of Deem Sum may be steamed at one time. Trays of the various types of dumplings, three or four to a plate, are then brought to the table and the patron may choose as many or as few as he wishes. At the end of the meal, the empty plates are counted and charges are made accordingly. Sharp "mustard," vinegar, and hot sauces of various kinds are also served to be used as condiments.

In the Chinese language, when words are put together to form a phrase, they take on completely different meanings. If you try to separate these words in translation, you will get completely lost.

"Foot (length) reading" means letter-writing, as a formal letter is written on paper a foot in length.

"Hand connecting" means procedure.

"Closed heart" means care about.

"Little heart" means be careful.

"Point heart" means snacks, and this sounds like deem sum, therefore deem sum means "snacks."

Deem sum is in Cantonese dialect, in Mandarin it would be Tien Tion.

Besides the two fundamental kinds of dough for deem sum (fermented and unfermented), there are also different amounts of fillings that can be used. There actually is a standard size for the filling, but it is very flexible and optional, especially in home cooking.

CHINESE SNACKS

This section also has too much variety and each province has its own style and customs. In general, snacks serve as breakfast, lunch, and afternoon tea. Their main purpose is to serve the morning worker too early to prepare a breakfast, and too far from home to return for lunch, and the agents and brokers who have a specific place and time where they have to meet their fellow friends for business dealings.

In northern and eastern China, tea houses serve only tea, and no more than half a dozen varieties of snacks. While Cantonese have twenty or more varieties, not including regular rice, noodles, cold meats, and dishes in miniature size, of snacks. Cantonese style snacks are appreciated by almost all Chinese of different provinces. On Sunday mornings or for noon teas, families usually bring their children to enjoy tea with snacks as a reward for good behavior.

One thing I would like to point out is that the Cantonese are very clever in selling their foods. They make their snacks in such small portions, and in so many varieties, that everyone will find something to his liking.

Northern Chinese will offer you only one dish. But Cantonese give you such a rare opportunity to have even shark fin soup of individual portion size, which is usually not served in smaller amounts than a twelve portion size, if it is for a dinner.

I have selected some from among hundreds of Chinese snacks which I wish you might make in your own kitchen. Your lack of equipment and experience are considered -- if you accept it as my consideration rather as an offense.

Steamed bun with stuffing: Generally, there are two kinds of dough. The unfermented is simple and quick to make, the dough is thin and firm. This size should be small, and the stuffings are various.

The only ingredients you will need to make unfermented dough are:

2 cups of all purpose flour
1 cup of water

You may use cold, warm, hot, or boiling water to make the dough. Knead it well to a soft consistency as dough for bread or pizza. Leave it aside in a covered container for at least 30 minutes before using it. Cold water will make the dough firmer, boiling water will make it softer. You can choose whichever you would like to use – don't forget you're running the show.

Fermented dough also has several methods for preparation. The best method is the worst for family use, unless you are going to use it every day, day after day. The most likely suitable method for you may be this: Wait! first let's understand the chemical function of fermentation. You need yeast to make the fermentation in a shorter period of time. Yeast is a biological product. It needs to be activated as it comes in a frozen state. It has to be at a warm temperature with some nourishment in order for the yeast to stay alive and multiply. Therefore, warm it with patience, do not boil it or you will kill the yeast. Nourish it with sugar and milk, don't add seasonings as salt will hurt the yeast also. Sugar and milk have another function in the preparation of the dough. Sugar will compensate the sourness of the fermentation, and milk will provide a whiter appearance and softer consistency. Many other things may be used instead of sugar and milk.

I like to give cooking instructions to people as human beings – not to program a computer. With all the reasons I explained above, readers should understand that there is a great range of possibilities in dough fermentation. French bread is one good example, the recipe is very simple, yet it is very difficult to make well. One thing I learned from Brazilian bakers is that the firewood oven plays a part in the quality, although the electric ovens are much easier to control the heat.

If readers think that a recipe with exact measurements is the only thing needed to make a dough, then they will be disappointed. When the result is not satisfactory, try to reason with all the information to check the mistake, and try it again. If someone tries to impress you with precision measurements in recipes, ask him to demonstrate with French bread.

Almost all the ingredients used in preparing a dough can affect the finished product a great deal:

All purpose flour: products from different regions and seasons make a big problem.

Milk: the fat content plays a part.

Sugar: this would be rather basically all the same. Check the degree of sweetness.

Lard: if you can make your own lard, it will be best. Ask your butcher for a piece of lard, it is not fat, it is like a piece of pure white pressed, glazed sugar. If you cannot use lard, don't use butter - it will spoil all the Chinese taste. Chicken fat can be used very well.

Yeast: if it is not spoiled, the quality is usually reliable.

Speaking about lard: let's make it the following way: Cut the lard into half inch cubes, add a small amount of water (about 1/4 cup per pound). Cook it under medium heat to a boil. Simmer and maintain the heat at the boiling point, without a lid, until the water is completely evaporated. Strain and keep the residue for cooking. Oh! A very simple dish will be enchanting by just adding the residue without any modifications -- steamed eggs (custard) is one. You can do the same with chicken and duck's fat. But these residues are useless. Lard will keep well in a cold place without sunshine, while the others will be better stored in a covered jar in the refrigerator.

Here is the recipe for making fermented dough:

4 cups all purpose flour
2 T. lard
1/2 cup sugar
3/4 regular small cake of yeast
1 cup milk

Mix sugar and milk with yeast. Keep aside for 20 minutes. Cut the lard finely into flour and add to milk mixture. Knead roughly, set aside for an hour or more covered. When the volume has nearly doubled, knead again and set aside for another 40 minutes.

Please note that a large amount of sugar is Cantonese style in the steamed bun. Northern style uses only 1 or 2 tablespoonfuls. This brings a slightly sour taste.

One more important thing to remember is after you fill the buns, before steaming, they should be stored aside, covered, for another 15 minutes.

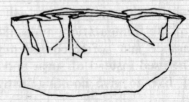

Some examples of fillings for use with fermented dough are:

Roasted pork, diced. Thicken it with oyster sauce, and cool before use to make the famous "Steamed Bun of Roast Pork."

To make this filling, first mince the pork and season it with 1 tsp. salt, 1 T. light soy sauce, and 1 tsp. sugar. Add 1 tsp. wine, 1 tsp. sesame oil, and 2 T. cold water per pound of pork. The minced pork may be mixed with chopped vegetables also for variety.

"Vegetarian's bun" is a delicious variation, but is usually more expensive. Here's what is used: Chopped vegetables (Chinese cabbage, etc.), dried bean curd, chopped, chopped mushrooms, transparent vermicelli cut into bits, hard-cooked scrambled eggs, chopped. Use all of these or only those that you like. When the filling has no meat, remember to use a lot of oil to make the bun more delicious.

Here are some examples of fillings you can use with unfermented dough:

Minced pork -- it is good with this dough also.
Vegetarian's filling is rarely used.
Roasted pork filling is never used.

Shrimps make a good filling. Mix shelled shrimp with the following (per each 8 oz. of shrimp):

1 tsp. salt
1 tsp. wine
1/4 tsp. pepper
2 pieces of ginger the size of a quarter, cut finely into threads
2 pieces of pork fat, cut into very fine bits

This shrimp filling is actually best for a dough made from wheat starch. I was very surprised to read that one cookbook says that you have to find "Dung Min," which is the Chinese name for wheat starch. The author said that there is no substitute. I never bother searching for wheat starch (it is very hard to find). Cornstarch is quite good. Some starches, such as tapioca, are not very good as they leave a noticeable smell. To prepare this dough, only boiling water should be used. This dough made from starch will have a transparent appearance, as does the famous shrimp dumpling above.

  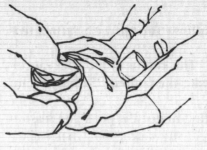 

1. For each bun, place spoon of filling on a piece of round dough.

2. Gather the edges of the dough up around the filling in loose, natural folds.

3. Bring the folds up to the top of the ball and twist securely together.

4. Set the bun aside with its twisted side up.

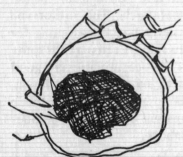  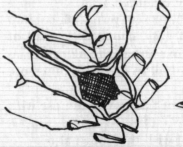 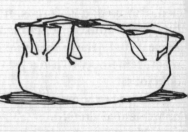

1. For each dumpling, spoon filling on a piece of round dough.

2. Fold the dough in half across the filling and pinch it together at the center.

3. Make 3 or 4 pleats at each end to gather the dough around the filling.

4. Pinch along the top of the dumpling to seal the edges tightly together.

The fillings for dumplings are too numerous to mention. One typical Shanghai filling is short grain rice, cooked with broth, soy sauce, a lot of seasoning, and lard. "Sealed folded dumplings" (the dumpling is well sealed at the edge), may use a gelatine filling. For this you may use chicken's feet, pork skin, etc. or just plain gelatine from an envelope. Cook the gelatine to make a seasoned sauce, chill it until it forms a jelly, then cut the jelly into little pieces the size of peas. Fold these pieces of jelly into the filling to make the sealed folded dumplings. The rest of the procedure is just the same as for a regular filling. But after you steam the dumpling, the gelatine will melt to make a sauce, this is the famous "dumpling-with-the-soup-inside." It is impossible to fill the dumpling with soup, but you can fill it with soup in jelly form. Interesting? This is only one little trick of Chinese cooking.

Seafood is usually used with the gelatine filling. This means crab and shrimp mainly. The sauce should be light in color and ginger should always be used with it -- eggs may be mixed in too. If you do not like seafood, you may use beef and mutton instead. When you use these meats, however, little variation can be made. I have tried and found out that to mix chopped onion in blends into a good filling with the gelatine.

Onion should always be browned and have a crispy texture and a good smell. If stuffed into the dumpling and cooked there, it will give a very strong unpleasant smell to the dumplings.

Knowing this about onions, I chop them first, and salt them with 1 tsp. salt per cup of onion. Then let the chopped onion stand for 15 minutes or more, rinse it with boiling water, followed by cold tap water, drain it

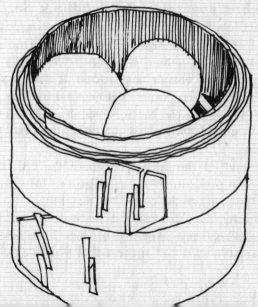

until dry, then fold it into the minced, seasoned meat. Use lots of sesame oil – the result is very satisfactory.

Sweet fillings can also be used, and there are a great number of them, here are a few examples:

Mashed red-bean. (Some call it bean paste. Puree is not an English word, "mashed" gives the name very faithfully.) Cook the red beans until completely soft. Now a wok is almost indispensible as you have to cook the soft mashed beans until they dry as, what the Chinese call, a "sand." Without a wok, this will be a difficult task.

Under a low heat, add in lard and sugar, in the ratio of about 1 : 1/2 : 1. The sugar will melt in. The moisture in the cooked beans should be evaporated slowly out, the lard will help in this drying process. If it stays shiny and doesn't stick when you are stirring and folding, stop adding the lard. When the batch is well dried it will keep for weeks in a cold dark place. Shape it into a ball to be used as filling.

The above is the way to prepare the red beans, using the same procedure you can also use lotus seeds, which are much more delicious, but also much more expensive. During the Mid-autumn festival, the Chinese mooncake-makers use a large sum of these lotus seeds.

For westerners, I can suggest that you use mashed potatoes. Make them on the dry side, adding a little essence oil. You may use many variations, using sugar of course. You may also tint the batch with food coloring. Always use lard, not butter.

Some ingredients used by Chinese as sweet fillings are: dates, tangerine peels, dried fruit, coconut, sesame seeds, watermelon, many other seeds, and a lot of nuts also. Rose petals cured in sugar make a good filling. Even though we have several dozen roses in our garden each day during the season, I haven't used them because they are sprayed each month with insecticide. If you have roses that haven't been sprayed, just separate the petals in a jar, mix them with sugar, and after several days they are cured.

To use this cured rose sugar, you need only to mix in lard, or even better, buy a piece of raw lard (or leaf fat), dice it, and marinate with the strongest not-sweet Chinese wine you can find. If you cannot find any, you can use 1 T. vodka per 8 oz. diced lard with 1/4 cup of sugar and marinate for a couple of hours or overnight.

One more thing I want to tell you is that when lard has been treated this way, its fat will not run. It becomes crunchy and maintains its volume, to play a part in the filling.

WON-TON SOUP

Prepare 4 cups chicken broth. Bring 4 cups water to a boil. Add in raw Won-Ton and turn heat to medium setting, bring to boil again. Add in 1/4 cup cold water to lower the temperature, allow to come to a boil. Strain the Won-Ton, add to hot broth and serve. Garnish with a few drops sesame oil and chopped green onion. Lettuce can also be added (See Lettuce Soup).

The deep-fried Won-Ton can also be added to the hot broth and served as a soup. In this case, however, be sure to fry the Won—Ton with fresh oil.

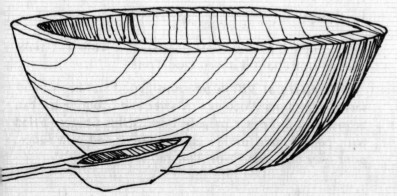

WON TON

Won-Ton is considered a snack by the Chinese. Most Westerners like Won-Ton, therefore, Won-Ton also comes as a soup for dinner. Won-Ton is a stuffed dumpling. Fresh lasagna dough is similar to the dough of Won-Ton, but much thicker. Home-made Won-Ton dough, although not difficult to make, is rather tedious. The dough can be made with pure eggs or half eggs and half water. If you live in San Francisco or a city with a large Chinese population, you can buy very good Won-Ton dough already prepared at a very reasonable price. The Won-Ton dough is sold by weight, it comes about 3" x 3" square, and is a flat piece of dough.

129

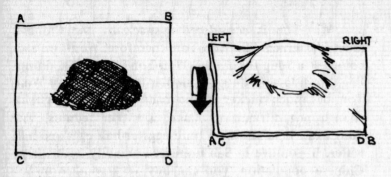

INSTRUCTIONS FOR FOLDING WON–TON

Instructions for folding Won-Ton:
Step 1 - Bring A and B to C and D. Press firmly with finger at edge, moistening slightly.
Step 2 - Moisten R. Press L to top of R.

Filling for Won-Ton

8 oz. pork - minced
1 1/2 T. light soy sauce
1 tsp. sugar
1/2 tsp sesame oil
1/2 tsp. wine

Combine all the above ingredients. This will make enough for about 3 dozen Won-Ton.

Deep-fry at 320 degrees until good and brown and serve as an hors d'oeuvres. A sweet and sour sauce can be used as a dip. Or prepare Pork Strips Chinese-Fried with pepper, add in 1/4 cup of sweet and sour sauce. pour over deep-fried Won-Ton and serve as a dish.

THE GENGHIS KHAN BARBECUE PAN

The Genghis Khan Barbecue Pan apparently derives its name from a similarity in appearance with the iron battle helmets worn by the Khan's infantry. Both are dome-shaped and have a flaired lip around the outside. There is even the possibility that damaged helmets were used as crude cooking instruments by the Mongolians, this inspiring the more modern version.

The design of the pan is such that very little fuel is needed. Quite possibly the Mongolians had an implement very similar to the ones manufactured today in Japan and Hongkong. The Koreans also use a similar unit made of brass.

Basically, the "Mongolian Barbecue" is an inverted cast iron pan. The cooking is done on what ordinarily would be the outside bottom. Ridges and channels are cast into the pan allowing fat and juices to flow away from the meats during cooking. There is a shallow lip or reservoir around the base where these juices collect.

The heat source is used to bring the entire pan to a high temperature, then thin strips of meat are "grilled" on the "surface". Actually what is being done is closer to frying with the juices from the meat running down

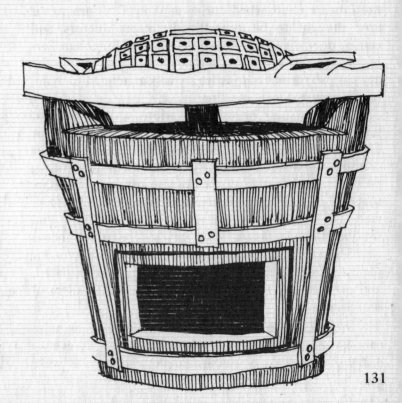

131

the channels away from the meat, producing a more healthful, less greasy, dryer result. Most "western" frying methods allow the meat to sit in its own juices, and the fats are re-absorbed during cooking. This practice is now thought to be unhealthy by many doctors, and causes poor digestion. However, on the Mongolian Barbecue, the meats do have a tendency to turn out on the dry side, so various marinades are recommended to maintain moisture during cooking.

The pan may be used in various ways. The most satisfactory method is outdoors on a small hibachi or Chinese charcoal stove. Most hibachis bought in this country are cast iron and are designed for simple grilling purposes. However, both the Chinese and Japanese manufacture clay or earthenware charcoal stoves. The stoves were originally used to support wok pans in China, and sukiyaki pans in Japan. They vary in size from 3 inches to 18 inches in diameter and are ideal heat sources for the Mongolian Barbecue Pan. They are heavily insulated, and may be placed directly on the table without fear of scorching.

Western style stoves may also be used to heat the pan. Since it is cast iron, the heat is more or less evenly distributed and gas or electric ranges work equally well.

There are "slots" or "holes" in most versions that allow small amounts of "smoke", when using charcoal, to enter the meat. No juices usually drip through these vents so the pan may be placed directly on the western stove's burner. However, some smoke from the food itself is normal, so a hood with a vent or fan is a necessity when using the pan indoors.

Some units have a larger reservoir around the base than others. This area may be used to simmer vegetables or partially cooked meats.

The care of the "Mongolian Barbecue Pan" is identical to any other un-coated cast iron pot. It should be allowed to season from cooking, washed gently with very mild soap and heat at low temperature until thoroughly dry. Care should be taken to clean both sides of the pan. The vent holes should be brushed clean on both sides. Since moisture of any kind will cause rust, a dry storage place is necessary.

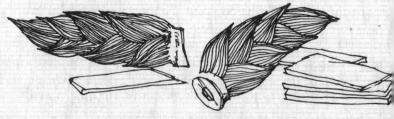

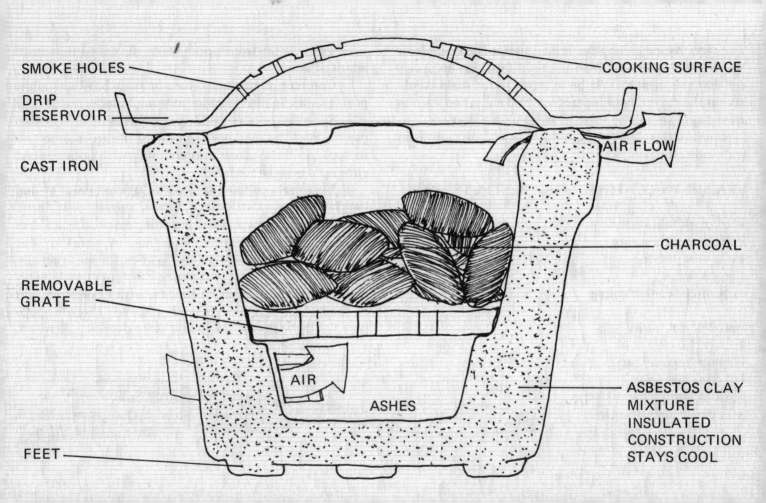

SMOKE HOLES

DRIP RESERVOIR

CAST IRON

REMOVABLE GRATE

FEET

COOKING SURFACE

AIR FLOW

CHARCOAL

AIR

ASHES

ASBESTOS CLAY MIXTURE INSULATED CONSTRUCTION STAYS COOL

Any recipe calling for grilled meats is adaptable to Mongolian barbecue. The only modifications necessary are that the meat should be in strips to facilitate handling on the curved cooking surface, and a method such as a marinade should be used to avoid undue dryness. Various meat strips, vegetables, and sauces may be combined with interesting results.

BRAISED PORK WITH WATER CHESTNUTS

2 lbs. pork loin steaks
1 can water chestnuts
1 can new potatoes
1 green onion
cornstarch for thickening

Marinade for pork:

1/3 cup light soy sauce
1/3 cup clam juice
1/3 cup Mirin wine or sherry
3 T. champagne vinegar

Trim all fat from pork steaks. Slice into thin strips about 5" long.

Combine all marinade ingredients in bowl and allow pork to soak in marinade for at least 30 minutes.

Slice the potatoes and water chestnuts in very thin pieces. Slice the base portion only of the green onion into medium-thick pieces and combine with potatoes and chestnuts in separate bowl.

Heat barbecue pan to medium high temperature and lightly braise pork strips until brown, turning constantly. When pork is brown, pour remaining marinade into drip channel around base and simmer the pork strips for 3 or 4 minutes. Have ready a bowl of rice for each person. Add potatoes, onions, and water chestnuts to meat and marinade in pan. Allow to heat through (2 or 3 minutes at most -- do not overcook vegetables). Thicken sauce very lightly with cornstarch and serve over rice. Serves 4.

BRAISED LIVER STRIPS

2 lbs. calves liver

Marinade for liver:

1/3 cup white vinegar
1/3 cup vegetable oil
3 T. clam juice
3 T. white wine
1 T. sugar
coarse ground black pepper
dash garlic salt
butter

Slice liver into strips and marinate for at least 30 minutes.

Pat liver strips dry with paper towel. Heat pan and melt butter. (The drip channel may be used to melt the butter also.) Brush butter over liver, then grill gently until very lightly done.

Serve with mashed potatoes and fresh peas. Serves 8

MEAT VARIETY DAH-BIN-LO

1 whole chicken breast
8 oz. lean, boneless pork
8 oz. top round beef
8 oz. pork liver, or chicken livers
1 dozen clams, in shells
8 oz. fillet of sole
2 oz. transparent vermicelli
1 lb. Chinese cabbage, trimmed
8 oz. spinach
4 - 3" squares bean curd, cut into 1/2" cubes
16 cups stock, strained

This recipe serves 8 portions.

Skin and bone the chicken breast. Cut into thin slices and use the remains for stock. Pork should be well trimmed, use trimming for stock. Beef trimming is not desirable for stock.

All the meats will be more easily sliced if chilled for 20 minutes in the freezer. Livers, after slicing, can be washed and drained, and the water used for stock. This will make a tasty stock, yet when served, the soup will be clear and the livers crispy.

The freshness of the clams is very important. Use

unopened clams of dollar size. They should be well washed with a stiff brush, and left unopened. The clams are immersed individually in water for approximately 1 minute. If the clams are indeed fresh, they will open like wings and the juices will further enrich the cooking broth. The wing-like shape of the freshly cooked clam reminds one of the ancient money of China, Yen-bow. It is for this reason that this particular dish is served during Chinese New Years as a portent of prosperity in the year ahead.

Fillet of fish should be sliced in strips, but not too thin (they break). Transparent vermicelli should be drained. (see guide) Chinese cabbage should be trimmed, use only the white firm part and cut into 3" lengths by 1/2" widths. The leaves can be used for making the stock. Spinach should be washed and drained well, then cut into 3" lengths. Fill the dah-bin-lo with the stock and add the bean curd at the same time. Keep the remaining stock warm on the kitchen stove, it will be needed later on when the broth is consumed as soup during the dinner.

In heating your dah-bin-lo or fire pot (if you don't know how to build a fire as a good boy scout should), here are some hints:

Charcoal briquets may be soaked with an inflaming agent and burned in a shallow pan, outside on the patio, or under the hood in your kitchen.

Your hair-dryer will give you the right amount of compressed air to help build the fire swiftly and effortlessly. If you like to work it in a typical Chinese way, blow through a tube – the original one is a hollowed out bamboo tube 3 feet in length.

You may also burn your fuel directly on top of your stove, or put it in a pan and broil till red hot. Transfer it to the dah-bin-lo, fill it with boiling stock, and bring it to the table.

Once on the table, you should not add any more fuel, as it makes a lot of ash. Therefore, always try to fill it full the first time. However, if you need more fuel, you may add it in carefully from the top. Arrange a piece of aluminum foil into a tubular shape with one end slightly bigger than the other. The bigger one will fit snugly over the chimney of the dah-bin-lo, the increased length will give you a better draft, and in seconds the fire will burn the fuel nicely.

In case the heat is too much, use any small fireproof dish or saucer to close the chimney. The heat will decrease immediately. Always leave a little margin, don't extinguish the fire completely.

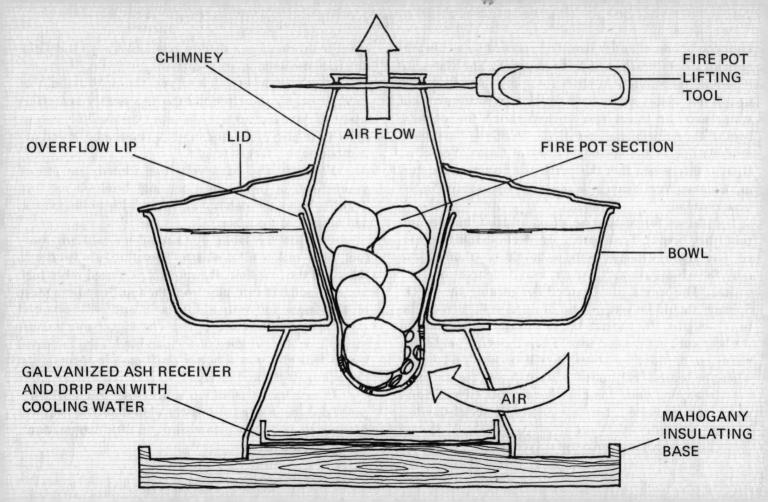

CHIMNEY

FIRE POT
LIFTING
TOOL

OVERFLOW LIP

LID

AIR FLOW

FIRE POT SECTION

BOWL

GALVANIZED ASH RECEIVER
AND DRIP PAN WITH
COOLING WATER

AIR

MAHOGANY
INSULATING
BASE

In serving, arrange all the cut meat and vegetables on small plates, so that they will be easier for everyone to reach. Start with the clams first -- this will increase the taste of the broth. You also may add a Chinese touch by saying "Kung Hshe Fat Choy" to your friends just before they begin eating!

The sauce to be used on the table is usually soy sauce mixed with a small amount of sesame oil. Oyster sauce, chili sauce, or oil may also be used.

Now give everyone a pair of chopsticks and allow them to each cook their own meat and vegetables by dipping it into the broth until done to taste.

Offer the soup in the dah-bin-lo at intervals, replenishing it with the extra broth from the kitchen. Each person is supposed to watch the cooking time for his meat or vegetables. Plain rice is desirable, although only a small quantity should be prepared.

The Chinese cabbage should be pre-cooked until done, and then drained. Sometimes, to control the heat of the pot, if it is rather too hot, you can ask everyone to immerse some cold cooked cabbage to decrease the temperature of the broth.

Spinach is very good for the dah-bin-lo, however, remember not to leave it in for too long as the soup will become dark and bitter. I personally would suggest that you always have everyone leave their spinach until almost the end of the dinner. Then have everyone immerse the spinach and have their rice to complete the dinner. Serve the last of the soup, leaving no time to let the spinach affect it. American lettuce is a wonderful vegetable for this interesting style of dinner, in which one pot holds everything.

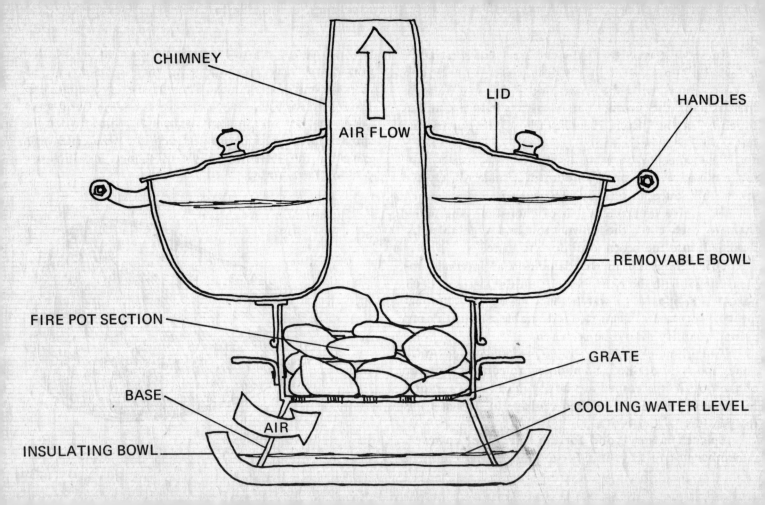

CHIMNEY

AIR FLOW

LID

HANDLES

REMOVABLE BOWL

FIRE POT SECTION

GRATE

BASE

AIR

COOLING WATER LEVEL

INSULATING BOWL

MUTTON DAH-BIN-LO

Mutton is consumed more in northern China, partly because more followers of the Moslem religion reside there, and partly because it is the region where a great deal of sheep are raised. Many eastern Chinese consider mutton to have too sharp or strong and heavy an odor, which actually is appreciated by those fond of mutton.

This is a very typical northern style dish for those fond of mutton. In order to let the taste of the mutton stand out, even the broth is plain water. After many platefuls of mutton have been dipped in the water, it becomes a strong mutton soup.

If you use chicken broth for this dish -- it is like adding Chanel No. 5 to a fresh rose. In Chinese we say: To show his drawing ability, he drew a snake and added four extra feet!

In northern restaurants, the mutton is sliced very thin, with no seasoning, and is served in a small dish the size for dessert. Enough water is added to the dah-bin-lo to serve all the diners. The waiter will bring you many different kinds of seasonings on saucers. Then, a dish of mutton is sliced for each diner. When (or sometimes before) you have finished your portion, which will never

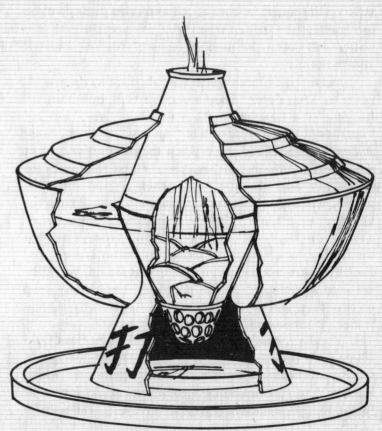

satisfy your appetite, the second and third dishes will be brought to the table. When you ask for the bill, the waiter will count the number of empty dishes, and tell you the sum.

Northern Chinese waiters are the best in the world, as far as I have seen. They are usually tall, but maintain the pose of a hunchback. They never say "yes," but say "yes, yes." Every customer is "big boss" to them. They always wear a hearty smile when they attend you. It is the practice only in northern restaurants that diners tip the waiter and also the cooks when a good dinner is served. When you do so, the waiter will shout in a voice like that of a tenor, "Fellow cooks, here are your rewards from big boss!" As the kitchen is always next to the dining hall, and no acoustic insulation is used, the cooks will never miss such a stimulating sound, yet, they are very accustomed to this practice. They calmly keep on working, and reply (almost as if directed by a band leader) at the same time, "Thanks, big boss!"

I really consider all these as sweet memories of old China. All professions deserve the same respect. It is worthy of pride to receive tips from customers which signify that you are doing a good service. As for those lousy, long faced, clumsy, inattentive, lazy waiters who would accept a penny dipped in syrup, yet never give you honest thanks, even if you tipped them heavily, they live on your tips, but are too cowardly to acknowledge it -- I suggest they find some other job! How many times dinners in restaurants have been spoiled by these kind of waiters.

You, readers, will never have to be a northern Chinese waiter, but you can easily beat them, I am very sure, if you are acting as host or hostess.

Use a leg of mutton, boneless, trimmed, and cut into thin slices. Allow at least 8 oz. per serving. (Don't be surprised if someone consumes several times more than his portion!)

Plain cooked and drained noodles are good instead of rice.

Bring the dah-bin-lo to the table, along with meat for each person.

Use several stalks of green onion per serving, cut into 3" lengths (green parts are not desirable).

Use seasoning of your choice: soy sauce mixed with a little sesame oil, chili sauce or paste, or oil. Red bean curd (fermented) paste, mashed with oil and with sugar added, can be used also. Or, you can blend all of these

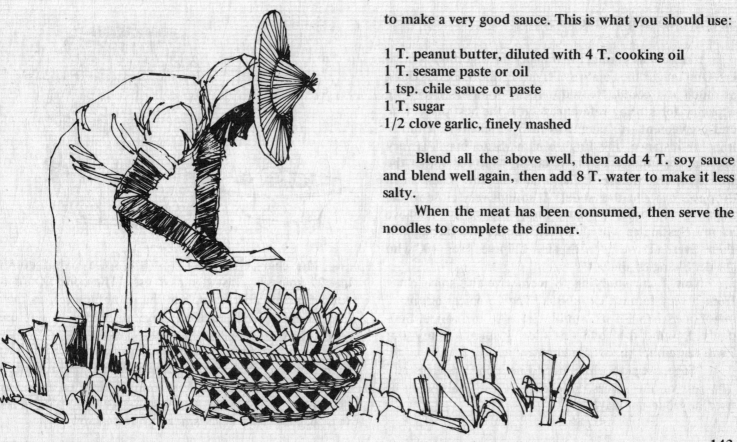

to make a very good sauce. This is what you should use:

1 T. peanut butter, diluted with 4 T. cooking oil
1 T. sesame paste or oil
1 tsp. chile sauce or paste
1 T. sugar
1/2 clove garlic, finely mashed

Blend all the above well, then add 4 T. soy sauce and blend well again, then add 8 T. water to make it less salty.

When the meat has been consumed, then serve the noodles to complete the dinner.

SOC'D AND YOUR SPICE CHART

When I was young, I had many unforgettable teachers. One taught me to always try to memorize everything as much as I could. He said that the brain has a very big capacity for storing references -- it is the best place, safe and convenient. He taught us many tricks for memorizing, for instance, the English name Scandinavia is very difficult for Chinese boys. He taught us to remember the words for this phrase: "The infamous King Yuen S-can dropped into a leather shoe!" It sounds very close to the name "Scandinavia", what a funny possibility! I believe all my classmates will always remember this throughout their lives. (Prove it with any Chinese over 40, who speaks Shanghai dialect!)

Now I am studying to memorize the spice chart from a very famous cookbook. The 13 spices against 7 major uses is a lot of combinations to memorize. Suddenly, I found the code -- SOC'd -- it sounds funny, but I will remember the whole chart by it.

"Sage, oregano, chile, not to be used for -- dessert." The rest of the spices, according to the chart, may be used anytime anyway!

The chart I received from the spice manufacturer has 21 spices against 8 major uses. The code SOC'd is good for this chart too, but the manufacturer, as they have more spices included, suggests that you not use curry powder, dill, and paprika in desserts!

There is a Chinese saying that some people talk just to prove that they are not mute. As a Chinese cook, I suggest that you don't use soy sauce, light or dark, soy bean paste, chile paste, oyster sauce, or shrimp paste for your dessert. And never smoke your dessert!

144

CHOP SUEY

It was only sixteen years ago that the first Chinese food restaurant was introduced in Brazil with professional cooks. Many good cooks were brought to Brazil by wealthy Chinese families. These cooks were tempted to get into the restaurant business. (The food quality in Chinese restaurants is very high.)

None of these cooks had had a chance to try chop suey. When they prepared their menus, they thought about this dish also, as it is internationally known.

To cook a dish without ever tasting or even seeing it is rather tricky. They studied it by the name, which must have some logical reasoning behind it, and descriptions by someone who had been to the United States. That is why the chop suey cooked in Brazil by Chinese is different from that served in the United States. But it was created by professional cooks, according to various rules in cooking, and I should say it is quite a good dish to be served.

Sao Paulo, Brazil, has 5 or more times the population of San Francisco, and only 5% fewer Chinese restaurants! What a big difference! It is also interesting to notice that almost everywhere where you find Chinese immigrants, most of them are Cantonese. In Brazil there was no exception in the beginning. But this time they did not get into the Chinese restaurant business in the same way as they did in the States. Therefore, the food from Chinese restaurants is not Cantonese style. As time marches on, everybody tries to enrich their cooking knowledge, gathering all the best, not bounded by provincial classification, now all kinds of dishes are served by Chinese cooks in Brazil.

Before the war, it was showing your character for a cook to specialize in only one style. Now, however, cooks will accept any order, if they know how to prepare it, which was considered an insult before if it was not their style. I think this is great.

It is my personal opinion that the chop suey made in Brazil is better. You can be the judge. To those cooks in the States, please don't get mad at me. Your success in the States is undeniable. Chop suey is still the best-seller in Chinese restaurants around the world.

145

PORK CHOP SUEY (BRAZILIAN)

Bean sprouts are supposed to be trimmed of all their roots. Place a big bowl or bucket of cold water in the middle of a table. Sit several people around each with a bunch of bean sprouts, trimming the roots one by one and tossing the bean sprouts trimmed into the water.

The water prevents the bean sprouts from becoming warm and also cleans them.

Drain the bean sprouts and keep them in cold clean water. They will stay good for several days in the refrigerator. When using them, take a small handful.

6 oz. pork, trimmed, cut into thin strips, and marinated
  with regular dark meat marinade
1/2 green pepper, trimmed and cut into strips
1/2 red pepper, trimmed and cut into strips
a couple of fingers of carrots, cut into thin strips

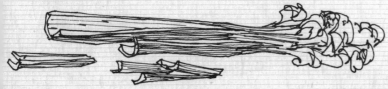

1 medium onion, cut into thin strips
a couple of fingers of bamboo shoots, cut into strips
a couple of fingers of celery, cut into strips
a couple of fingers of trimmed bean sprouts
1 T. soy sauce
1/4 tsp. salt
1 tsp. sugar
1 T. wine

Begin the Chinese-fry by first adding a piece of ginger and 1/2 clove of garlic. When they are browned, take them out. (You only need their flavor.)

Start with the pork strips first, when they are about 1/2 done, add the remaining strips, except for the bean sprouts. Keep on Chinese-frying (add soy sauce, salt, and sugar at this time also) until done.

Add in the bean sprouts, cook for no more than 10 seconds, add the wine, and thicken with a little cornstarch (the vegetables will give enough liquid for this). Add several drops of sesame oil, and serve.

This is a very colorful dish, you will have:

Red, green, white, yellow, and brown. The meat is tender, and it is not pre-roasted. The seasoning is well blended in.

PORK CHOP SUEY (AMERICAN)

This recipe was coached by telephone from a Cantonese friend of mine. He and his three brothers own a chop suey restaurant.

6 oz. roast pork, cut into thin strips
3 oz. onion, cut into thin strips
3 oz. celery, cut into thin strips
3 oz. bean sprouts, use as it comes to you
a piece of ginger, or
1/2 clove garlic (optional)
1 1/2 T. soy sauce
1 tsp. sugar
1/4 cup water or broth
1 tsp. cornstarch for thickening

Chinese-fry the onion, celery, and bean sprouts till done. Add in soy sauce, sugar, water or broth, and thicken with cornstarch.

Serve on a plate garnished with cut roast pork on top.

Frankly, this dish was invented very well, according to the demand. It is quick and the cost of labor is high. It is tasty, too.

Now, see the difference between American style and Brazilian style chop suey (by Chinese cooks, of course).

AGED AND FROZEN FOOD

Conserved eggs and cured hams all are very much more expensive than in their original form. All of them have a certain preserving limit, once passed, they will lose their quality.

The only frozen product which Chinese really like is perhaps ice-cream. I have known very few Chinese families who consume frozen vegetables. From the Chinese point of view, the time and effort spent to prepare fresh vegetables is the same as that spent to heat a pack of frozen vegetables. The vegetables are always less expensive and they always taste better.

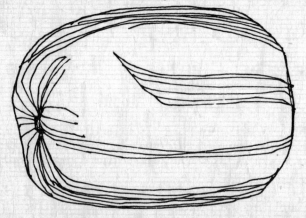

WATERMELONS AND HOW TO CHOOSE THEM

When choosing a watermelon, look for the following things:

The surface of the skin should not be very smooth, somewhat lumpy is better, but too lumpy is overripe.

As for the weight -- heavy is raw, light is ripe.

The navel should be deep.

Hit it with your fingers as for a chest examination. High pitch is raw, low pitch is ripe.

There is a kind of melon in China called "Horse-bell-melon." It is small and shaped like a horse's bell, very sweet, and orange in color. In the beginning, I did not believe it when the vendor held the melon to his ear, then told me it was a good melon! After a friendly question, he told me that he was not joking. By holding the melon with both hands, pressing or squeezing it somehow near your ear, you can tell if it is ripe. If it makes no sound at all when squeezed, it is raw, if it produces a slight crushing sound, it is just ripe. How clever were those secrets of each trade!

The easiest and surest way is to cut the melon in half, scoop out the middle, and taste it - this way was invented by my daughters!

Speaking about watermelon, when it is not sweet enough for eating as a fruit, you can still have the value of your money from the juice.

There are many ways to obtain the juice, for instance using a blender or squeezer, however, if you don't happen to have either of these in your kitchen, you can do it like this:

Cut the melon in half and put it over a large bowl (cut side up). Pierce a hole down through the melon and rind for drainage with a chopstick. Then scoop the melon from the middle, cutting it into small bits with a spoon. Then mash the bits of melon with a potato masher, removing the residue as it is used. Occasionally the hole in the bottom of the melon may become blocked -- you can unblock it simply by forcing a chopstick down through it again. You can use all the melon down to the white part.

I have found out that this juice is the best to follow a heavy drink. It also has a very nice aroma. You may add sugar also if required.

The white hard part of the melon is very good for cooking. Scoop away the soft part and cut away the green outer rind. Diced into 1/4" x 1/4", this white part is excellent for soup, especially if it is winter melon. The texture of water melon is even firmer, and the aroma is just wonderful. Cook it with chicken broth, diced chicken, giblets, diced roasted pork, shrimps, mushrooms -- and you have a luxurious soup from what you used to throw away.

The white part and the skin, cut into big strips, can also be made into pickles by immersing it under a sufficient amount of soy-bean paste. After a week or so, bring it out, wipe it dry with a paper towel, and cut into smaller strips or dice it. Add some sugar and sesame oil, and it makes very appetizing pickles to accompany plain rice congee. Only middle aged eastern Chinese will have tried this dish during the hot summer. This recipe may remind you of what you are missing now!

If you are really going to make these pickles, here's how: Wipe the white part of the melon dry with a paper towel and keep it in a windy place overnight. Wipe it again before immersing it in soy bean paste. After the pickling is done, the paste should be cooked thoroughly and kept for later use as seasoning.

Everybody is writing a cookbook, you don't need a license or qualification. You can write for pleasure or profit. I am writing partly for a longing for the old times that will never come back!

149

HOT AIR AND CHILLING FOODS

Lichee have been mentioned many times by famous poets. One well known poet was, Soo-sak of the Sung Dynesty, he said, "I wish to be a life-long Cantonese, eat daily 300 lichee."

Unfortunately, this verse was misinterpreted because of a difference in dialect. Some people, even now, insist that a famous saying came partly from this verse. The saying says that "Each lichee has 3 bunches of fire!" Fire is hot, and hot is "hot-air" — not the one from the room heater — and "hot-air-foods" are not recommended for children or even adults by some Chinese.

I hope you have some Chinese friends who can answer your questions about hot-air. He or she will give you a long list of hot-air-foods. Also, the opposite of hot-air, a list of chilling-foods! (Not related to the temperature of the food, but the nature of the food.) Please don't ask more, even you will certainly be puzzled! It is quite possible that there are some who know how to distinguish the hot-air and chilling-food, but they know no more than a list.

I am a very curious man. When something puzzles me I always like to find the reason why. I always believe that there must be a reason. Some examples of hot-air-foods are: fried chicken, or anything deep-fried, dried lichee, roasted pork to roasted peanuts, and hot spices, of course. Some chilling-foods are: sea weed, some green vegetables, and green tea, especially Dragon Well or Lung-chin, or Chrysanthemum tea.

I mention all this for a purpose. First, if the reader is a westerner, if serving a tea of some food to a Chinese, it is best to first find out if the guest cares about hot and chilling-foods. Second, I wish that some of my countrymen would please not stick to their eating habits. Because, by restricting your stomach to certain foods, you have already trained it not to accept others. If it is too late for you, please at least don't train your children in the same way. Let all of us grow healthy and more resistant. These foods were explained to me satisfactorily by a Cantonese doctor, who participated on the team that treated the first man to use an iron lung. Dr. Chou told me that foods regarded as hot-air are somehow not easily digested, which is good when a diet is required, but not for daily life, and the chilling-foods have a very slight, if any, laxative effect, which may help, but never hurts.

Thanks also go to Dr. Chou for giving me a good

answer to my question about why Cantonese use this traditional dish for the mother soon after labor — pork's feet with ginger, sugar, black beans and vinegar. He gave me this answer — This dish gives sufficient calcium and protein, is easy for digestion, and ginger and vinegar have the effect of relieving pain and healing.

Dr. Chou also stopped my asking why Cantonese like to use some medicine, steamed with chicken, to make a chicken broth with a medicinal smell. Most of us know how, but not why. Dr. Chou said: The proteins mixed with the medicine make it more easily absorbed by the internal systems. The chicken is not tasteful anymore, but this is not a dish, but rather a nourishing medicine the family way.

I hope that my Cantonese friends will be proud to have such a man as the Cantonese Dr. Chou. I also sincerely hope that my Cantonese friends will change their attitude toward hot-air and chilling-foods.

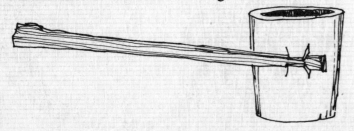

CHINESE AND WINE

It was recorded that when the first batch of wine in China was presented to the ruler, Emperor Shun, in the year 2000 B.C., he said, "Some day a nation will be destroyed by this stuff."

Wine has been commented on many times in Chinese history, and many beautiful poets have dedicated themselves to writing about it. One of the best poems, with modifications to suit English rhyme, goes like this:

Among the bushes of flowers, with wine in a bowl,
I am sipping alone, without even one companion.
I raise my hand to invite the moon, standing near
a tree,
With shadow of mine, moon, and me, we are three.

It seems like whenever Chinese have wine, they like to sing a song or recite a poem. Wine is used for celebrating, for drowning sorrow, for remembering a parting, for almost every occasion.

"Please take another cup of wine with me,
You are leaving westward, no more old friends such
as we."

151

When attanding a wedding ceremony dinner party, almost all Chinese provinces, although in different dialects, say: "I am going to drink," or "I am going to eat (Shanghainese) happy wine." It is obvious that the wine is more important than the food in such a celebration.

The old fashioned wedding party was a very noisy one. The host and hostess, generally the mother and father of the groom, were very satisfied if everyone made a lot of noise during the dinner party. Therefore, a game was born — "Finger Guessing." Two players show a certain number of fingers at the same time, accompanied with the shout of a number which they believe will be the total of all the fingers. They keep on trying until one hits the correct number, then the other is the loser. There are 11 possibilities of numbers, from zero to ten. As the Chinese like to use lucky words for any occasion, each number in the game will be shouted with a fancy touch such as "3-stars-shining-upon" (happiness, prosperity, and longevity), "4-seasons-of-good-business," "5-times-the-champ," 10 is substituted with phrases like "home sweet home."

A "good hand" or "good fist" means an expert player. By using a loud and strong voice, you can somehow scare your opponent. If you notice that he has a favorite number that he has a habit of repeating, 3 for instance, use different fingers each time yourself, but always add 3 to it and call this number to make a hit, as soon as the 3 appears you will eventually win the game. Many times you can make a direct hit on the first try. Stick your arm high in the air with fingers firm as iron, motionlessly as if you were sure to hit his numbers — this will really discourage your opponent, he will make a mistake in guessing, and you can easily beat him in the next match. In previous times, it was very important to be good at this game, as the loser was supposed to finish his drink. In this way it was very easy to reach your drinking limit while the party was still young, as everyone is expected to challenge all the other guests at the same round table (12 in total) and accept their challenge in return. Not everyone can drink so heavily so a known non-drinker was always excused, and only had to take a sip or even use a soft drink instead of wine. Also, as many times happens, charming girls and ladies were obliged to sing a song or do a dance to pay their obligation. After all, a party is for having fun, not for embarrassing anyone.

When the opponent is a new friend, if you win you should say, "Thanks, you let me win." If you lost, you should say, "What a good hand, thanks for teaching me."

Yes, Chinese are very polite people, and now let's see how intimate friends are talking before a match . . . .

"Hey, you rice-pot and wine-skin, dare you match yourself with me?"

"I will beat you as easily as I take something out of my pocket!"

"It takes miles to prove a horse, and seconds to prove that you are just nuts!"

"To beat you is like catching a turtle in a jar!"

When you lose a game, you must never lose face, this is what you can say . . .

" A gentleman never wins the first match!"

"What is wrong tonight, is the moon rising in the west?"

"I am thirsty, this is just fine for me to warm up!"

"What a big improvement, my dear pupil!"

When good friends are gathered, it is lots of fun. One famous proverb goes like this, "With your intimate, a thousand cups of wine is very little, with whom you don't like, half a sentence is too much talk."

Most Chinese drink their wine warmed to body temperature, while westerners use room temperature as a guide for some types of wine. Many stronger Chinese wines are as thick as liquors, but not sweet. Many sweet fruit wines are usually mild.

Japanese custom says that the guest should hold up his cup when the host is offering a second helping. Chinese also use this custom, but you may leave your cup on the table, and hit the table near your cup with your fingertips — this means "I am bowing."

DESSERT IN CHINA — THE LICHEE

For many people, a dinner without dessert is unfinished. I have never heard of a typical Chinese family serving dessert after dinner, other than fresh fruit. Only in a very formal dinner or at an occasional feast is dessert served.

There are many Chinese desserts which are very expensive and time consuming to prepare, such as the "Bird's Nest" and the "White Cloud Fungus."

There are also a number of desserts which are very difficult to prepare, such as the famous "3-Non-Sticking" dessert. This is made of egg yolk and sugar and should not stick to the cooking pan, the chopsticks, or the teeth — hence the name.

A fancy dessert? Oh! yes, my dear readers, one Chinese dessert imitates a peacock. It even uses watermelon seeds to imitate the texture of the peacock's feet! What else in details for a fancy dish can you ask for!

The mainland of China lies almost entirely in the temperate zone. Only portions of the three southernmost provinces — Yunnan, Kwangsi, and Kwangtung (Canton) — are within the tropics. For this reason, in these zones there are many tropical products which are not found in other parts of the country.

Lichee is one of the famous tropical fruits of the southern provinces. This fruit, besides the variety as to size, color of the shells, texture, sweetness, and size of the pits, also has many different kinds of fragrances. It is really a marvelous fruit which can also be sun-dried for yet another variety to be used as candy or in dessert cooking.

It is a fact that now the canned lichee from Taiwan is much better than that from the mainland of China. As a canned fruit, I think that it keeps much more of its original taste than many other canned fruits. I am sure that the westerner can easily adopt this fruit to be used in many fancy ways as a dessert. As I am Chinese, I still believe that the best way to serve it is slightly chilled, or you can also warm the juice and add in the fruit before serving as a warm dessert.

In 1954, a Portuguese gentleman who'd been raised in China, a Sr. Xavier, spent a tremendous effort in bringing twenty five thousand lichee plants to South America. Most of them did not resist the long journey, part of them did survive, however. Although he may only produce one specimen yearly, I hope his effort will keep going strongly forever. During my newly married life, I

was fortunate enough to be living in the region where lichee is produced. My wife and I will always remember the nights spent after our dinner, sitting on the stone bench still warm from the day's sun, under the banyan tree, shelling a bucket of lichee. They were fresh every day, and we don't believe there could be any way possible of conserving that flavor and texture, with all the food processing knowledge known.

The lichee was mentioned in history during the Dong Dynesty. The Emperor Ming-juan kept a beautiful mistress named Yiu-wan (Kwai-fi). She was recorded as a woman with a perfect body. She was supposedly so beautiful, that her name is now a standard nickname for beautiful women.

She was easily bothered by the hot summers in her palace located in the center of China near the Yellow River, and liked to have a lot of fresh fruit. The Emperor therefore ordered his subject to form a pony express to bring fresh lichee from the southern provinces — a thousand miles away! In this way assuring that his mistress would have fresh lichee daily.

A GUIDE FOR YOU

BAMBOO SHOOTS - Use only the unseasoned kind from Taiwan. If refrigerated, don't keep them too near the freezer, this will spoil the texture. They will keep well for weeks if covered with water and a lid, change the water twice weekly.

BEAN CURD — Use the harder type for stewing or Chinese-frying, the soft type for soup or steaming. See section on bean curd for storing.

BEAN PASTE - This is the base for making soy sauce, therefore, it has a stronger soy taste. As it is salty, sugar should always be used accordingly.

BEAN SPROUTS - Mung bean sprouts are smaller and good for use as a garnish. Chinese-fry them only. Soy bean sprouts are bigger and good for stewing and soups. The former should never be overcooked, while the latter is just to the contrary.

BEEF - Use top round, keep the trimmings for stewing. Flank steak will leave useless trimmings and it can only be cut vertically across the grain, thus it cannot be cut into very big slices. Knowing how to marinate the beef, you will never need to bother buying filet mignon.

BLACK BEAN (fermented) - They will keep well for months if stored in a dry place. Rinse them thoroughly with tap water before use. Always mash them with garlic to form a paste. They should be browned slightly in oil to bring out their flavor.

BONES - Gather your bones until you have a sufficient amount for a broth. Or, when you need them, ask your butcher to sell you some pork bones. If there is a delicatessen near your area that sells Italian style food or Virginia ham, he might supply you with a ham bone. Accept it if the price is very low, because when the ham becomes a bone, the owner has already pocketed a good profit! Ham bone is best for broth. Don't use too much, ask him to cut the bone into 6 or 8 pieces and keep some for later use. Always parboil the bones before making broth.

CHICKEN - Most supermarkets have a reasonable supply at a reasonable price. If you want a fresh, trimmed chicken, you can easily find them in San Francisco to be used for a crispy fried chicken.

CORIANDER - This is a foreign herb and was developed in China. Its Chinese name clearly shows its origin in the West. I thank people for giving this herb the name of Chinese Parsley.

DUCK - A small duck has little to offer. If a big duck is too much for you, you can buy half a duck in San Francisco.

EGGS - If the number you use daily is more than 4, you should consider buying eggs in 2 1/2 dozen packages. Whenever a recipe calls for egg whites only or yolk only, always prepare another dish using eggs, and add the leftover yolk or white to that dish. This saves you the effort of saving the leftover egg and you can spend the time searching for another dish to cook!

FISH - Use filet of sole for deep-frying with batter, use cod or a similar type (whole) for stewing or for sweet and sour cooking. Use only fresh fish for steaming or poaching. Use ready-made fish meat for balls or cakes.

GINGER - Ginger root is always used in seafood. Many times it can be used with garlic. If fresh ginger is not available, you can use ginger in powder form.

INTERNAL PARTS - Many bargains on good meats can be found if you accept these kinds of meats, which are usually delicious and good for a dieter, e.g. hearts, kidney, tripe, etc. Someone said that the first man to eat a lobster must have been very brave. If you don't accept them because you have never tried them, then you have really missed a delicious dish at a bargain price. Not many recipes in this book deal with these meats. I wish I could complete it with a more interesting collection, however, the disadvantage of these meats is that they are comparatively tedious to prepare.

MUSHROOMS - If you buy them in a bag, use the bigger and smaller ones for slices and strips, and keep the uniform medium sized ones for stewing, etc. Dried mushrooms should be soaked in water — the longer the better. Keep the water for sauce, etc.

NOODLES - Don't buy the pre-fried type, they might have a rancid oily smell. Any Chinese brand is less expensive and very much better. Use the thin ones for noodles in soup, the coarser or wider ones for frying.

OIL - Peanut oil is by far the best for Chinese cooking. Never use butter or margarine. If you use vegetable oil, be sure it is not made from cotton seeds — this gives a strong smell. The new products for deep-frying add only a strong smell and heavy weight to fried foods. You cannot even drain it, and although it seems less greasy, the shortening stays with the food. If you would like a bargain, buy oil by the gallon can, it never spoils. Why don't you?

OYSTER SAUCE - This is a dark brown sauce which comes in a bottle. It is made from oysters, clams, and soy sauce, cooked and condensed with starch. Use it as a dip, as with cold poached chicken, or for a sauce. Use it 1 to 1 with soy sauce, and add the same amount of water with a little more starch for thickening.

PORK - Some butchers sell tenderloin of pork, and at inexpensive prices. This is the best cut to use for Chinese-frying or steaming. Pork chops are rather expensive if they are going to be trimmed and only the meat used. Leg of pork is quite good for general use, expecially for mincing.

RICE - Once again, why not take advantage of a bargain? Buy rice in 10 lb. or more bags. If you ever calculated the price per ounce, you would see that buying oil and rice in small packages is very costly.

SESAME OIL - Only Chinese manufactured sesame oil will give you the special aroma, as refineries might produce an odorless oil. Remember that this is the last touch for almost every dish. Most cold dishes also need the oil to give them a delightful flavor.

SOY SAUCE - Light in color (or raw) should be used in light color cooking, while the dark (or old) is for stewing and Chinese-frying. Sugar should always follow soy sauce, although in a very small quantity (to blend the flavor, not to sweeten).

STARCH - Cornstarch is quite all right for thickening in family use. It is more expensive than tapioca starch, which is stronger in consistency.

TRANSPARENT VERMICELLI - This is made from the starch of mung beans. It should be soaked in cold water before use. Bring it to a boil, cover, and set aside for 30 minutes. Drain and use in Chinese-frying, stewing, or soup.

WINE - There are many very good Chinese wines as most of them are produced on the mainland of China. The difference between them and other wines is that they are thick, as a liquor, very strong, but not sweet. Here are the names of some Chinese wines: Kaoliang Spirit from the northern provinces, Fen Liquor from Shen-si province, Dai-cheu from Szechuan province. Green of bamboo leaves from many provinces. Mau-tai from Kwaichow province. These are regarded as the top 5 Chinese wines.

WHERE? - If you cannot find anything in your area, go to Chinatown — they have more than enough for you. People in San Francisco sometimes do not know how to profit by going to Chinatown. It is like passing by a cave full of treasure without going in to pick out some precious pieces. This is the biggest Chinatown in the western hemisphere, and you shouldn't miss it.

HOW CONFUCIOUS EATS HIS DINNER

The Great Master must have been a gourmet and a dietician. It is amazing to discover how much the Master mentioned food to his disciples and most of his words are still correct by modern standards:

There is never too much caprice in cooking.

No discolored food, badly flavored or badly cooked food should be eaten. No out of season food should be eaten.

Meat should be cut properly and served with the proper sauce.

You should eat a well balanced meal with the proper proportion of meat.

Never buy already cooked food.

When a dish calls for ginger, never omit it.

Don't deliver a speech during dinner.

My translation is not direct but the original would be a puzzle for you to read. Although the Great Master never had a refrigerator I am sure he would advise you to keep all leftovers in a refrigerator. I am quite sure that if the Great Master had only enough money to buy a TV set or a refrigerator the Master would have chosen the latter. Not everyone has his intelligence and therefore many families have a TV set only.

162

CHINESE TABLE MANNERS

Generally the old time table manners were much more formal than they are now. Now when you are asked to be the guest of honor, you accept with sincerity and thank your host for the honor. In the old fashioned times the host and guest of honor would fight for at least two minutes, the guest being expected to at first refuse the honor. This was considered a sign of politeness and humbleness. At last he would accept after much persistence by the host. Now we have a modern opinion that to obey and accept is an indication of honor and respect for the host.

When each dish is served, the host should point with his chopsticks to the plate but should not touch the plate and use a simple word as "please" which means, please help yourself first, and a friendly smile, of course. The guest should reply right away with the work "thank you" and not hesitate to pick out his portion otherwise the host would have to wait for him.

As most dishes are cut in small bite sizes, don't take too large a quantity to avoid having to leave a portion on your plate in case you don't like it.

When you are invited to have a second helping of something which you don't particularly care for you can say "oh, thank you but I very much enjoy . . ." and name another dish which you do like and have some of the other dish.

The Cantonese feel that the last single piece of food on a dish should be eaten by no one while the northern Chinese would offer the last piece to the guest of honor as a sign of respect. He is expected to accept However, do not ask a Cantonese guest of honor to have the last piece. Even many Cantonese don't know the reason for leaving the last piece of food. There are many taboos in Chinese conversation and the word which means "single" sounds very much like the word for "alone" and for "poison" and since the word is taboo, the last single piece of food is also taboo. Another taboo is the word "empty" and for this reason an empty box will be referred to as a "good box." The taboo concerning the last piece of meat is sometimes solved by waiting until there are two pieces of meat on the plate. One person at the party will invite another to eat and they will each pick up one piece at the same time so that there will be no last "single" piece.

PRACTICE MAKES PERFECT

This title is too common for English speaking people. But I would like to tell you a story which was recorded in Chinese. Before you will understand the story, one thing must be explained. When I was a boy, cooking oil was sold mostly in bulk. The oil vendor used a meassuring ladle, he had several sizes, to fill the bottle of the buyer using a funnel. One day a professional archer was shooting. The archer hit the bull's-eye three times consecutively and felt very much content, but the watcher, the old man who vended oil, was not impressed at all. The archer was bothered and asked the old man if he could do it. The old man answered simply, "No, but I can do something which I doubt you can." The old man calmly lifted a ladleful of oil and with another hand held a Chinese coin which had a small hole in the middle and poured the oil through the hole of the coin into a bottle. He spilled no oil and the coin remained untouched. After the old man finished the pouring, he commented flatly, "This is nothing but some practice."

Perhaps we can never be perfect in anything, but we can certainly better anything by practicing. If you like to cook, practice it more. And I hope you will be a better cook — I am still trying.

Thank you for your patience in reading this till the end. Any questions, corrections, suggestions will be sincerely appreciated and answered. Please enclose a stamped envelope.

Everyone is offering a guarantee when selling something. I guarantee that this book will give you complete satisfaction or YOU will be returned to the same you, without any questions asked.

My sincere hope is that you find something useful in this little book. I wish to write for you again.

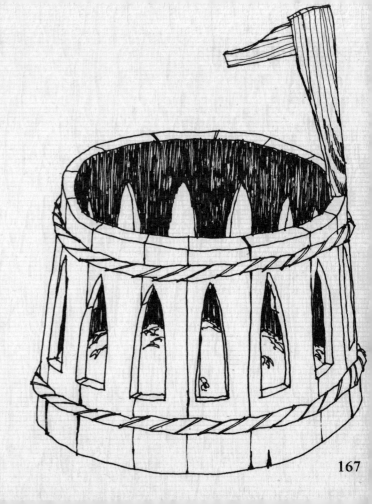

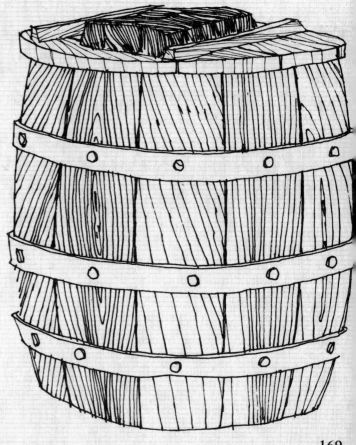

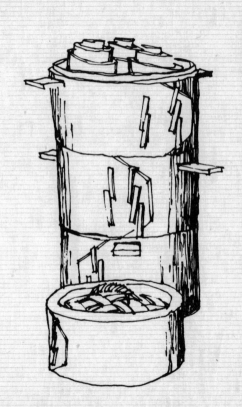

INDEX

173